I AM' ARRESTED

Victor Krone

Copyright ©

All Scripture quotations, unless otherwise indicated, are taken from the Holy Bible, New Living Translation, Copyright © *1996, 2004, 2007, 2013, 2015 by Tyndale House Foundation.* Scripture quotations marked (+) are taken from the New King James Version ® Copyright © 1982 by Thomas Nelson Inc.

Used by permission. All rights reserved. Scripture quotations marked (MSG) are taken from The Message. Copyright © by Eugene H. Peterson 1993,1994,1995,1996,2000,2001, 2002. Used by permission of NavPress. All rights reserved. Represented by Tyndale House Publishers Inc

I Am' Arrested
Copyright © Vic Krone 2019

ISBN: 978-0-6486888-6-0   Paperback
ISBN: 978-0-6486888-7-7   E-book

All rights reserved. Without limiting the rights under copyright reserved above, no part of this publication may be reproduced, stored in or introduced into a database and retrieval system or transmitted in any form or by any means (electronic, mechanical, photocopying, recording or otherwise) without the prior written permission of both the owner of copyright and the above publishers.

Photographs by Dennis Curran.

Published with the assistance of angelkey.com.au

DEDICATION

I dedicate this book to Lindy, my wife, soul mate, best friend, and prayer partner who not only celebrated the highs and endured the lows during the writing of this book but also through our shared journey of Christian ministry and doing life together; you have been a constant support who has always affirmed me and believed in me. You have accepted me unreservedly. You have loved me to the moon and back. I thank God for you.

ACKNOWLEDGMENTS

Bill Magher (Billy the bricky), a mate and brother in Christ who was bold and fearless in sharing his faith with me. I remain eternally grateful to you for introducing me to Jesus Christ.

Ian Kruithoff for being a friend and mentor, who has been a steady guide with a firm, loving hand for Lindy and me, through the many years of ministry.

Euan Malia, a faithful friend, thank you for your honesty and wisdom and being a sounding board with the big issues of life. (Especially your home-cooked fish and chips)

Jurgen Wiesner, thank you for being there through our early years of ministry in particular Bible College; you were there for me, believed in me, and encouraged me.

Charmaine Sime, thank you for your tireless work and the many hours editing and rephrasing my manuscript your creativity and writing prowess has made it readable and relatable.

CONTENTS

Endorsements vii
Foreword (by Pastor Graham Shand) ix
Author's Preface xi
Introduction An Excerpt. xiii
Chapter 1 - Aussie Battlers 1
Chapter 2 - My Firsts. 13
Chapter 3 - Work, Booze & Family 19
Chapter 4 - The Road to Hell. 35
Chapter 5 - The Road to Freedom 43
Chapter 6 - New Beginnings 51
Chapter 7 - Doubts at the River Jordan 55
Chapter 8 - Never Alone 63
Chapter 9 - Learning, Growing & Serving 79
Chapter 10 - Southampton Revisited. 95
Chapter 11 - Change & Prophecy 103
Chapter 12 - Passing the Baton 113
Chapter 13 - Growing Pains. 125
Chapter 14 - Family. 131
Chapter 15 - I AM Arrested! 135

ENDORSEMENTS

In this book, you will read about not so much Vic finding God as God finding Vic. The persistence of God and the responsiveness of Vic combined to produce a great story of restoration and transformation. Vic's journey is inspirational as he and God turned his life around. He went from a life lived for himself to a life of service to others. He went from pub to pulpit.

His is a story of new things. He found a new life. He found new love. He found a new purpose. This book shares how this happened for Vic, and how it can happen for anyone. The stories may be different, but the way to a transformed life remains the same.

Ps Ian Kruithoff
ACC Victoria Church Growth Director &
ACCI Relief Board Member

To say that Vic Krone has had a major turn-around in his life is an understatement! As a long-time friend, (18 years), I have seen Vic in many different circumstances, and it's hard to imagine some of the stories and experiences contained in this honest portrayal of his life. For me, only having experienced the nothing but gentle, kind, humble, and 'servant-hearted bloke,' to then hear about 'Before Christ Vic', is like hearing about a stranger.

As a psychologist and previously, a dual diagnosis senior clinician (drug and alcohol/mental health), I am very much aware of the unusual swiftness of Vic's recovery and change in character and values. I can only attribute this change as a great testament to the power of faith, and God's loving pursual.

Andree Sellars
Psychologist MAPS

Vic is a very humble man whom I've known since I was ten years old. I never saw the man that his kids knew way back then because He's *not* the same man they know now. I've only ever seen the man who loved on the alcoholics, the lonely, the broken-hearted, and the downtrodden at any time of the night or day. I saw the man who could paint, repair and fix anything!

I now see Him love His wife greatly and serve God with all that He is. I see him cheer people on no matter their past. I see his great love for all his family praying for them always. I believe God is very proud of His Son Vic. I believe he has an amazing story that all can appreciate. May it change your life!

Ps Charmaine Sime

FOREWORD

I so valued reading Vic's real life account of the transformation that he has experienced – taking him from some very dark seasons to a place of hope and significance.

There is an air of authenticity to his story that is relatable and inspirational. He brings hope that no matter how far we have sunk amid our circumstances, God can and will bring us through as we place our confidence in Him, not as an event but more-so in taking progressive steps with the support of key people in our life.

Finally, there is a real sense of destiny to his story- that our lives are not simply a series of random events, but rather, God has a plan that is yet to be revealed.

Graham Shand (Lead Pastor)
Aspire Church (formally Casey Life Church)
Web: www.aspire.church

AUTHOR'S PREFACE

This is my story, as I remember it. I have stepped out of my comfort zone so that you might be encouraged. If God could sort out the chaos of my broken atheistic life, He can do the same for you.

I had no idea how challenging it would be to write this book, not so much because of my inexperience as a writer, but as I began to recall some of the shameful things I had done, combined with the regret of the things *I could have done* during 18 years of alcoholism it began weighing heavily on me.

The nagging voice of condemnation in my mind was very convincing', saying, *'look what you did you're guilty! Look what you have missed out on, you're a loser!'* Admittedly, for a time, this robbed me of joy and peace of mind. But God is faithful, and once again, reminded me that my past does not dictate who I am. I pray my story will be a great reminder that God has a plan and purpose for you no matter what your past! Your past does not dictate who you are.

INTRODUCTION – AN EXCERPT

I didn't see the truck coming. To this day, I don't remember the details of the event, but I do remember the look of anguish on my mother's face as she re-lived that historic moment all over again. Time stood still as she began to speak.

It happened so fast! Mum lifted her eyes from her smiling boy, but too late. My mother was powerless to do anything, but see this awful nightmare come to pass right in front of her eyes. It would only last seconds, but to her, it felt like an eternity.

The speeding truck complete with a drunk driver and large front bumper bar, connected with her little boy, throwing me metres away from her. I was head high to the front bumper bar, my face taking most of the impact.

The force of the impact caused severe head and facial lacerations that would forever leave its scar. In a heartbeat, I went from a lively and energetic toddler going for a walk, to a motionless, bloodied bundle of pulp on the side of the road. The truck driver eventually stopped but was so drunk he could barely stand up straight.

I should have died! But God had another plan!

Chapter 1

AUSSIE BATTLERS

On the 7th of December 1941, America entered World War II. Australia quickly became a strategic base for the US, with an estimated one million of its military personnel in Australia by the end of December 1941.

The US military was stationed mainly in Northern Australia, but Melbourne had its fair share of US military, as well as the many Aussie diggers who were camped on the iconic Melbourne Cricket Ground, waiting for further deployment.

There were many fistfights because the American soldiers were more popular with Australian women than the Australian soldiers. They had plenty of money and access to nylon stockings, chocolates and cigarettes, and other luxury items unavailable to the Aussie military.

It was with this backdrop that Patricia (Pat) Maidment, a gorgeous green-eyed blonde, worked as a waitress at the Oyster Bar, a well-known seafood restaurant in Melbourne's CBD.

Pat had met and became lifelong best friends with 'Aunty Lorna', an attractive brunette. Lorna had come to the big smoke from the small Victorian country town of Eldorado near Wangaratta. They became roommates and would often go out on double dates with service members who flooded Melbourne during the war.

These were exciting times for a couple of good-lookers like Pat and Lorna, as they learnt to jitterbug and jive on the packed dance floor of the Trocadero or go ice-skating at the Glaciarium. They watched the many wartime movies, with Charlie Chaplin as *The Great Dictator*, Tyrone Power in *A Yank in the R.A.F.*, *Buck Privates* with Bud Abbott and Lou Costello or the iconic *Casablanca* with Humphrey Bogart and Ingrid Bergman.

Pat and Lorna had plenty of proposals from the many US marines, but both fell in love and married Aussie servicemen. Lorna married Sunny, and Pat, well she would go on to marry Maurie Krone, a handsome cheeky sailor who was back home in Melbourne after having been deployed to Darwin, Northern Territory, which had been under intense Japanese aerial attack.

It was a chance meeting under the clocks of Flinders Street Railway Station. "I was with Aunty Lorna," Mum said, "and we were pushing our way through the crowd when we heard a wolf whistle. It came from a man I recognised from a previous double date when he was with another girl. He stopped right under the clock and asked me out on a date. I said, yes!" Mum and Dad fell in love and married in 1946.

On the 28th of November 1948, I came along—Victor Charles Krone, Mum's first child and a baby brother to Dad's first son, a 13-year-old, known as, 'young Maurie', my big brother. Just over 12 months later, a baby sister, Lynette Marie Krone, arrived. Lyn was born on the 9th of December 1949.

Things were financially tough in Australia just after the end of World War II, and there was only Dad's wage to keep our growing family. To help mum and dad save for a deposit on their own home, we lived at Nanna Krone's house in Port Melbourne. It was crowded, as my cousin Leo Ryan and his wife Faye, stayed there too.

Chapter 1   AUSSIE BATTLERS

Nanna Krone's house was a double-fronted terrace with a small front porch behind a Brunswick green wrought iron fence. The front door opened into a passageway that went straight through to the back door, with rooms on either side. It was during this time on a beautiful autumn day in Melbourne in April 1950, that an accident would occur that would mar my toddler body forever, but more of that later!

Our family was typical of most working-class families after the Second World War—the husband went out to work while the mum stayed home with the kids. Dad worked at the West Melbourne Gasworks as a stationary engine driver, (a fitter in today's terminology).

He managed to scrape together and borrow enough for a deposit to buy their first home—an old Victorian house that was almost derelict. It had a stable to one side at the rear and a cobblestone drive with back lane access. The stumps and bearers had rotted out, and it was sitting on the ground.

It was typical of the type the old Victorians built in the 1800s—14-foot (4.26m) ceilings with pressed ornate tin and ornate cornices and ceiling roses. It had 12-inch (30cm) skirting boards with a six-inch architrave around the doors. It had sash windows with a passage that went from front to back with rooms either side. If the front and back doors were open on a windy day, the doors would slam, and you'd hear someone yell, 'Who left the bloody door open?'

The Smith family lived next door. Theirs was a large family with ten kids, mainly raised by their mum. They were poor—the kids in rags with no shoes—and they always looked like they needed a wash and their hair combed. They got up to lots of mischief.

Early one morning, they found a man asleep on the footpath at the front of our house. He was one of the local drunks who hadn't made it home. He had a nearly empty bottle of cheap wine lying beside him. The Smith kids, being full of cheek, said to Mum, 'We pissed in his wine bottle.' They thought it was a great joke! Mum wasn't impressed. 'Leave the poor bugger alone.'

She had great empathy for down-and-outs but wouldn't put up with any threat to her or the family. Maurie told me, once when Dad was on a night shift at the gas works, an intruder came up the side way with an axe over his shoulder.

Mum challenged him. 'What do you think you're doing?'

'I'm looking for Bill Smith!'

'Well, he's not here', she yelled with great authority, and the intruder quickly turned around and trudged off into the night.

Mum was a kind-hearted, brave lady with streetwise discernment who had learnt to survive during the depression in Melbourne. She and her young brother, Uncle Charlie, never knew their real dad. He deserted them at a young age, leaving them to be raised by their mum as a sole parent.

Mum's family were honest hard workers but heavy drinkers who wouldn't go looking for trouble but wouldn't back away from a blue. They were larger than life characters who I looked up to, and my admiration would show in my life actions later.

Grandfather Charlie (Bluey Mathews), Mum's stepdad was a tough little bloke who had belonged to the Ninth Australian battalion, which was the first to set foot on Gallipoli. He had been wounded and taken prisoner by the Turks. Before the war, he'd been a sheep shearer and a professional boxer.

Nanny Millie met and married Grandfather Charlie when Mum and her brother were in their late teens. Mum said that he loved and provided for Millie, who was a big lady with a big heart who loved her kids, grandkids, and great grandkids too. She had a saying about her size— 'Once around Myers, twice around my waist.'

Chapter 1   AUSSIE BATTLERS

Uncle Charlie, Mum's brother, was a big bloke with green eyes and thick waves of blonde hair. He was a happy-go-lucky character who had little or no schooling. He grew up during the Depression years and knocked about the city.

At one time, two young blokes picked a fight with Charlie, nicknamed Hippo. He picked one of them up and dumped him in a horse trough near Queen Victoria Market. The other bloke took off in a big hurry.

Uncle Charlie joined the army and was shipped off to the Korean Peninsula with the Third Battalion of The Royal Australian Regiment.

After the Korean War, he returned home to a lifestyle of heavy drinking and partying, spending his time and money in the pubs around the city of Melbourne. He could handle himself in a barroom brawl. On one occasion, he was attacked with a broken beer glass and lost an eye.

East Bentleigh

In 1953 Mum and Dad finished renovating their house and moved from the city to East Bentleigh, a developing suburb. There were market gardens, unmade roads, and new houses were being built with a thunderbox down the backyard, which was serviced by the night-man.

Horse and cart delivered milk, bread and ice. There were new schools, lots of kids and pregnant mums and my new baby brother, Ross Telling Krone.

I learnt at least *one* thing at East Bentleigh State School, and I learnt it the hard way! It taught me not to claim something that wasn't mine. Metodius (Meto), who was my first friend, was involved. He was raised by his Albanian dad who had migrated with him to Australia after World War II from war-torn Europe. His German mum had died just after the war before making it to Australia.

Monday morning at a school assembly, we would stand together and sing *God Save the Queen*, which was our national anthem at the time. Then there were some announcements, including any lost property handed in, and you put your hand up if it was yours.

'Sometimes it's money,' said Meto. 'Just put your hand up and say it's yours then we can buy some lollies after school.'

It was a shilling (about 12 cents), good money when you were in grade two in the 1950s. But it didn't take much investigation from the teacher to realise I had lied and got my *first* strap across the hand. Ouch!

Our new house in East Bentleigh was opposite open land, which eventually became Bailey Reserve. It was a great area for us kids to muck around exploring and playing.

One day as I ran down one of the large mounds of dirt, one of the older kids shot me in the chest with a slug gun. It didn't break the skin but left a bad bruise. I was lucky he didn't go for my head, or I might have lost an eye.

We also had a bonfire there for Guy Fawkes Night. The community put out all their combustible rubbish and lit it up on the fifth of November with crackers and other fireworks.

At other times we climbed into the unfinished houses or sneaked under the fence of the many market gardens to pinch some carrots. We washed them under the new house's tap and munched away.

With the babies 'booming' and the many migrant families arriving in Australia, along with the housing boom, many new schools had to be built. Our new school was Valkstone Primary, which was in a straight line over Bailey Reserve from our house.

My big brother, Maurie, left home after marrying his childhood sweetheart, Shirley, and built a new house opposite the school. I thought it was fantastic having him

Chapter 1 AUSSIE BATTLERS

so close. I bragged to the other kids because he was big and had tattoos on his arms. Most times he was at work during the day but occasionally, he was home, and I would eat my lunch with him and Shirley.

Maurie was a wharfie and very quickly learnt to fit into the sub-culture on the waterfront. It was in the days before containers when ships carried cargo in crates, boxes and were manually loaded and unloaded. Maurie started there at 15 years of age, obviously putting his age up because the legal age was 21. I would later go on to use the same trick.

One day on a walk home from school, after yelling at pretty Irene, 'You're silly anyway!' I was set upon by her big brother, Peter, who was in sixth grade and the school bully. Unfortunately, my big brother wasn't available. I came home with blood all over my clothes.

Mum was upset to see me in such a state. After cleaning me up and consoling me, she gave me a glass of milk and a vegemite sandwich, which was a great tonic for seven-year-old Victor! 'We've got to teach Victor how to defend himself. We don't know how much more his head and badly scarred face can take,' said Dad. He had done a bit of boxing and self-defence.

Grandfather Charlie was ex-pro boxer, and big brother Maurie had learnt to look after himself on the waterfront, so between them, they taught me to not only defend myself but to punch offensively. Eventually, I got a speedball and heavy bag for training, but they kept me away from any competition boxing for fear of any brain or further facial damage.

My first bicycle was Dad's Malvern Star three-speed. He repainted it and put on new tyres and hand grips. It had been his transport to work when we lived in South Melbourne, as only a few families had a car in the years just after the end of

World War II. But by the early 1950s, the economy started to build, especially with the huge influx of migrants.

Dad taught me to ride my renewed bicycle and instructed me not to leave it lying in the dirt but stand it up against a wall or the curb. I didn't want to get dirt in the peddles so, after I gained confidence, I proudly rode around to the shop to get something for Mum and stood my bike up in the gutter with one peddle on the kerb in front of the milk bar. When I came out, there was only a mangled mess, as a delivery driver reversing into the shops hadn't seen it. I had to wait until the following Christmas to get a brand-new bike.

With many long hot summers and what seemed an endless supply of fresh water, we played under the sprinklers, made water slides or squirted each other with the hose. We thought nothing of hosing down a driveway or concrete path. Visitors from the country could hardly believe how wasteful we were, as they only had tank water.

If we weren't playing in the backyard with water, we would be off on our bikes and would ride down North Road to the Brighton seawater baths or over to the Oakleigh Olympic-size swimming pool. Mum would give me a shilling, which was enough to get in and buy lunch and a drink. If we had any pennies or halfpennies left over on the long ride back home, Meto and I pleaded with the man at the fish and chip shop to give us some chips with salt and vinegar wrapped in newspaper for threepence.

Our house, along with others in our area, was built on ex-market garden land. We had beautiful black sandy loam soil in which to plant gardens and sow lawn. It was my job to mow the lawns with a push mower, which I enjoyed, I received two shillings for it.

As my sister's birthday approached, I thought I'd buy her a box of chocolates from the local milk bar. They were nine shillings, and I had paid them off on lay-by. Mum and

Dad knew and must have been proud that I was doing this for my sister. After the last payment, I had managed to secrete them home and put them on the top shelf in my wardrobe. The temptation came to try just one. It was fantastic! I had another and another the whole box was gone! Mum said, 'It's Lyn's birthday today, Victor!' I still feel guilty when I think of the chocolate box of empty wrappers. Sorry, Lyn!

In November 1956, while running flat out pushing another kid's bicycle, I tripped and fell on my left knee. The council were in the process of sealing our road, and the sharp loose stones cut me to the bone.

Dr Alan Rose was our family doctor. He was also a skilled surgeon. My knee was so bad he had to perform a skin graft, taking small sections of skin from my thigh above the badly injured knee. The doctor had planned to see some of the Olympic Games events in Melbourne at that time but was held up to work on my knee.

It was just before my eighth birthday, and we couldn't afford a television, but our neighbour three doors up had one and let me sit up to watch a black and white television for the first time, showing the Melbourne Olympics. I felt very special.

The Milk Bar

It was just before the end of the third term at Valkstone Primary School. I was in grade six with Mr Hogan, who was my favourite teacher. He got the best out of me in the classroom and encouraged me in my passion for sports. He sometimes let some of us come to school early and get out the sporting equipment and kick the footy or play tippity-runs cricket.

Dad built a garage from second-hand bricks, established all the gardens with concrete paving, and even built a dollhouse for Lyn from a wooden car crate. Being multiskilled, he started a part-time cabinet making business. Mum worked part-time serving in a fruit shop after Ross started kinder, and Nanna Krone sold her house in Port Melbourne to come and live with us in East Bentleigh.

Mum felt strongly about going into a business. After Dad agreed and, seeing the potential of being able to stop working at the gas works, he started looking around for a business but needed a residence with enough room to accommodate Nanna.

He eventually found one in Pascoe Vale. It was bittersweet for me, as I had to leave my friends and school, but the thought of being in our milk bar with all the ice cream and lollies helped us get over the loss and make new friends.

Our arrival in Pascoe Vale was just before the last term of the school year, which meant we finished our primary school at Pascoe Vale Primary.

Lyn and I served in the shop after school and on weekends. It was a mixed business with fruit, vegetables and groceries. Dad had a green Vanguard panel van and purchased groceries from the wholesale market and purchased fruit and vegetables from Queen Victoria Market.

On Saturday evening he travelled to Diamond Creek to purchase fresh bread to sell on Sunday, as it was illegal to bake on Sunday in the city and suburbs of Melbourne in those years. It's hard to believe that considering today's trading hours, but this was before the introduction of supermarkets and large shopping centres. We only had strip shopping, which closed on Saturday afternoon until Monday morning.

I still cringe when I think back on one time when I served in the shop, and a customer asked for a packet of lady's sanitary napkins for his wife. I didn't know what they were. 'What are these for?' I asked. The man had a puzzled look on his face and turned to Dad, who had also heard my question and stepped in to finish serving the shocked man.

Chapter 1   AUSSIE BATTLERS

All Dad said was, 'Always put them into a brown paper bag for the customer.'

One of our regular customers took an interest in me, giving me tennis lessons on Saturday mornings. On one occasion she and her husband asked if I would like to go to church with them. I remember having Holy Communion, so I think it was an Anglican church. I was 13 years old and didn't know what it was about, but now as a Christian, I realise God had been there for me.

In 1961, Australia experienced a credit squeeze which didn't help business sales. The council remade the road in front of the shop, so there was no passing trade and Nanna Krone passed away.

Looking back through my life experiences, I imagine these would have been challenging times for Mum and Dad, as they had to try and sell the business with low sales figures. They must have lost a lot of money because we moved back to East Bentleigh to an old weatherboard house and they had to find work and try and build up again.

I started secondary school at the all-boys Coburg Technical School and later enrolled at Moorabbin Technical School (another all-boys school) after we moved back to East Bentleigh.

On my first day, one of the tough kids picked a fight with me. I defended his punches and didn't land any on him, but I did gain some respect from the other boys after that.

I was often in trouble with the teachers. Big Jack Sorell was our sheet metal teacher and caught me egging on a first former who was fighting a bigger kid. I was going to give him some tips but ended up with six of the best with big Jack's feared thick leather strap. That hurt! And Mr Willox was our music teacher who had a special weapon—a triple-layered Lino strap. Once again for fighting, he gave me six of the best for me, but at least this time the other boys copped it too.

Our home in East Bentleigh was a rundown ex-housing commission house, but it was all we could afford after the failed milk bar business. Dad started working at Streets Ice Cream in Holmesglen as a fitter and Mum did process work in a factory in Moorabbin. They worked hard and slowly built up their finances until they could afford to put an extension on the house, build a garage and renovate the rest of it.

The Hamburger Shop

Mum still felt strongly about going into a business and took on 'The Hamburger Shop'. It was a coffee lounge during the day, with a steady flow of customers, and sold hamburgers, fish and chips, and cold drinks of an evening. It attracted a lot of youth.

The shop was diagonally opposite the East Boundary Hotel in East Bentleigh. Hotels closed at six o'clock in Victoria at the time, and the patrons placed their last orders at six and had to drink it before 6.15 pm; known as 'the six o'clock swill'. Some ordered up to 10 glasses and tried to scull them down before 6.15 pm. Consequently, there were lots of fights and words of abuse, especially on a hot day.

I had what was known then as a typical Aussie upbringing. Looking back, I recognised that God had his hand on my life far more than I thought. Psalm 139: 1-10 says (paraphrased) that God sees and knows and is familiar with all our ways. We don't always recognise it at the time, most often we see it in hindsight. But faith is not hindsight; faith is believing. Know that God purposed your life, and He sees you right in this moment, your struggle, your strife. You are never alone!

Chapter 2

MY FIRSTS

My first job was at ROK Steel in Moorabbin, erecting office and shop shelving. By this stage, I was not going to school anymore, and this job paid five pounds per week. I was 14 years old.

I started smoking and wanted to do what the older blokes did, that included going to the pub and having my first beer with them. But I was underage and couldn't legally purchase alcohol, *but that didn't stop me for long.*

I remember the first time I tasted beer. I thought it was horrible. But in a drinking school at the pub, I learnt that you don't sip and taste beer, you scull it down for effect. I soon developed a taste for it though and the effect!

After the pub closed at six one night, (when I was still new to the effects of drinking sessions), I staggered home and in my drunken state, became aggressive and punched some young man for no reason. The police were informed, and I was charged and convicted with assault. It was my Dad who arranged legal representation and being underage I was fined but not given a record.

Dad had taught me to drive in his 1959 Holden FC when I was 14 years old. We would go into the country on a rabbit shooting trip, and he'd let me have a go on a country lane or paddock. When I was 16, my Dad bought me a 1952 Austin A40. He got it cheap, as the motor needed rings and bearings, but it was drivable, and in those days that's all that really matters for your first car.

I remember feeling so proud of driving around and showing my friends my very own car. The trouble was, not only was I unlicensed, I would start with one beer and then go on a pub crawl. I can't remember much of my *first* drink-driving binge, but I did manage to get home to my parents' house. With my impaired parking skills, I drove the car up the gutter, over the nature strip and ended up on the front lawn. As the car stopped, the driver's side front wheel fell *off,* and as it leant over, the driver side door opened, and I fell *out*. My parents found me lying on the grass, blind drunk.

Dad organised for his mate to take the car away and recondition the engine. When it came back, he warned me not to go over 35 miles per hour, (about 56km), until I had run in the reconditioned motor. However, I took three mates and went driving all day up to Healesville back across to Mornington Peninsula to Portsea and back down to Dromana.

We thought it would be a marvellous idea to drive onto the Dromana Pier. It took about 20 goes to turn the old Austin around at the end of the pier. But that wasn't enough adventure yet, so we headed toward Frankston.

As we passed the mile bridge at Frankston, heading to Seaford, I joined my three mates who had fallen asleep. The problem was, I was the one driving!

The car veered to the wrong side of the road and slammed into a front fence and gate. My knees left imprints in the dashboard, causing bad bruising, but the other three, while being rudely awakened, were unhurt. One of my mates in the car had a driver's licence and said he'd tell the police he had been driving. With the stupid act of drunk driving *and* driving too long without a break, I wrecked my first car. 'Hey Dad, I did run it in!' *Seriously, I look back and thanked God that no one was hurt.*

When I was around 15, I started getting into trouble with the police. My friends at that time were older and involved in petty criminal activity. Some had served short-term prison sentences. I was with them, breaking in and stealing cigarettes and cash from petrol stations, stealing cars for joy rides.

We also stole petrol by milking cars, which involved siphoning them with a piece of garden hose. I put the siphon in the tank and started sucking up with my mouth, then let gravity do the rest. Many times, I got a mouth full of petrol.

There was one time I was glad I hadn't gone out with my friends. They picked up a couple of teenage girls and did the wrong thing. They were charged with rape and spent a few years in prison.

What road was I heading down? My life consisted of two goals. Do what the other blokes did and make it to the next beer! I couldn't see it then, but I was heading down a dangerous road.

With the hope of getting me away from this criminal element, Dad sat me down to tell me that after an accident that had nearly killed me as a child and had left me permanently scarred, I had been awarded £1000 damages, which was being held in a trust account until I turned 21.

This amount had accrued interest and, when converted to decimal currency, was $3500. In 1969 this was a lot of money. This news, along with Dad's sagely advice, kept me from a potential prison sentence.

Phillip Morris and My First Girlfriend

In 1964 there was plenty of work available in Victoria. I could walk into the office of any company and ask if they had any vacancies. Security screening and curriculum vitae checks didn't matter. Anyone could go under a false name and put his age up to 21 to get full adult wages.

I had little education; I hadn't finished year nine, so was always working as a labourer or in a factory. What better place to work than a nice clean factory that gave a cigarette ration as well as good adult wages?

The only thing they said at the interview was that we were only to smoke Phillip Morris cigarettes, and they must have been good for you because the advertising line was, 'Why not try Phillip Morris plain? You've nothing to lose but your smoker's cough.'

By this time, I had plucked up enough courage to ask a pretty girl out on a date. Jean was sitting with some other ladies having lunch in the Phillip Morris diner. After noticing me, she smiled, which gave me enough encouragement to walk over there and ask her out. She said, 'Yes, but I will have to ask my mum.' Much to my delight, her mum said yes, thinking I was a *responsible 21-year-old*. After all, I had lied about my age and said I was 21.

The lies eventually caught up with me. After we had had a serious romance for 12 months, Jean became pregnant. When her mum found out that I was the 'culprit', she rang my mum and was concerned because I was supposedly 21 and her daughter was only 16. Mary (Jean's mum), was further appalled when she heard that I too was only 16 because I had been giving her husband, Tom, driving lessons in his yellow vanguard while not being old enough to have a driver's licence myself!

My parents encouraged me to stick with Jean and the baby and sought an underage marriage licence, but was denied. They then engaged a barrister and eventually, we had legal permission to marry.

To help support my wife and baby son, I continued to lie about my age which enabled me to gain full adult wages, and I started working on the garbage trucks at the Moorabbin Council. I had a second job in the local pub as a barman and the bottle shop.

Chapter 2 MY FIRSTS

On my first day on the garbage pickup, the 'garbos' lined up outside the gate at around 5.30 am, waiting for the overseer to open up. I remember noticing some old Garbos drinking beer and wondered how they could drink then work. It didn't take long for me to join them. My whole life once again revolved around alcohol, and I loved it!

Looking back, I thank God that my Dad stepped in when He did. He was trying to instil in me a hope and a vision for my future. To help me see that life had far greater value than how I was living and to try living for more than just that drunk moment.

I had nearly died when I was a kid, and how many more times would I cheat death? My Dad tried using money to motivate me at least to aim to make it to my 21st birthday. I don't think even he'd imagined that by then I would be married with a baby and still be an alcoholic

I know now that my heavenly Father also has a plan. Jeremiah 29.11 says "I know the plans that I have for you. Plans to prosper God has a greater future for us than we can ever dream." If only I had stopped and appreciated what was going on then. If only I had...

Do you have any 'if only I had moments?' Where are you in your life right now? My encouragement to you, make the changes now. There is hope; you are so valuable that your heavenly Father has a plan for your life. He values it.

Sadly, it would be some time before I would truly come to know this.

Chapter 3

WORK, BOOZE & FAMILY

When working as a Garbo in the sixties and seventies, there were three men per truck running each side, picking up the rubbish and sharing the driving. It was also the early days of recycling, so the residents left their empty beer bottles beside their rubbish bins. We would empty the bins and bag up the bottles in reusable hessian bags. They were hung on the side or rear of the truck until they were full, then tied up with tile wire and often thrown on the roof of the garbage truck in stacks.

Occupational health and safety weren't implemented then, and the stacks on the roof of the truck could be four high and involved two Garbos being on top of the truck while it was travelling to the tip at speeds of up to 80 kilometres per hour.

Most of the blokes were fit, in their twenties and thirties and usually, had a second job. Many of the blokes were tradesmen and would go back to their trade as part-time butchers, mechanics, gardeners, delivery drivers or pub workers – like me.

I eventually did come of age and finally got around to getting a legal driver's licence. I wouldn't hold it for too long, though. Around this time, I was pub fighting and drink-driving, sometimes, with family in the car. Being arrested, being locked in jail, then fighting in jail was a common occurrence. I lost my licence for drink-driving and was charged with assault, stealing, lying and starting a chainsaw in a public bar with the intent to terrorise.

I also entered the beer glass chewing competition in the public bar of the Southside Six Hotel; involving biting off pieces of glass down as far as possible. Amazingly, I didn't cut my mouth!

I had violent outbursts with threats. I was obnoxious and used blasphemous foul language from which most people would walk away. On one occasion, I was so drunk I had double vision but still wanted to keep drinking. I asked the barman if he could make me up something that would sober me up so I could drink some more. He suggested I go home. I wanted to take him outside and fight him.

Milk Delivery

I spent five years working on the garbage trucks and doing various second jobs, including milk delivery with a horse and cart from the Bentleigh Dairy. This job was traditionally hard to get, but it was just before they started phasing out home milk delivery, and the writing was on the wall for many long-serving milkmen.

I started after some basic training in harnessing the horse and loading the cart. I learnt the round, although the horse knew it and would stop at the various homes by himself. My horse, Trigger, was slow and laborious when starting with the cart full of milk but was in a hurry to get back for a feed.

Even though my second jobs changed often, my life of alcoholism didn't. One day after my latest drinking session, I headed off to work still full of alcohol and thoroughly exhausted at 1.30 am for my 2 am start. I headed off from our home at Mulgrave and stopped at a red light at the intersection of Warragul and Centre Road, South Oakleigh.

Unknown to me, I was at that intersection for over an hour – I had blacked out. It was reported that some other motorists had tried to wake me and thought I was dead. Eventually, I regained consciousness and drove to the dairy.

Waverly Rubbish Removals

I decided to stop working on the garbage trucks and start working for myself. I didn't know anything about running a business that, at the very least, would have to generate enough money to pay the mortgage, support my family and support my thirst for alcohol.

After purchasing a second-hand dodge truck with a flat tray and a new McCulloch chainsaw, I placed an advertisement in the local paper calling myself 'Waverley Rubbish Removals', including tree lopping and removal.

One time the public trustees asked if I would quote to cut down and remove a large cypress tree. They gave me the OK for the job, believing I was an experienced tree lopper, which I was not. It was a massive tree on the front of a property in Brighton. I had asked Maurie to help on his days off, and we had it down and taken away within a week.

Amazingly, neither of us were injured, and no surrounding property was damaged, which was a stroke of luck because some of the massive branches were over powerlines and neighbours' homes.

I received payment from the public trustees by way of a cheque, cashed it at the bank, paid my brother and headed for the Moorabbin Hotel. I had over $1000 in my pocket, which for me, was a lot of money in the early 1970s.

But my ferocious thirst for alcohol took over, and I fronted up to the public bar and ordered the *first* two 10-ounce pots of icy cold beer. Hours later, once again, the police arrested me. I was on the bonnet of my truck and lying spreadeagled on my back, having fallen asleep in a drunken stupor. When I was arrested, the pub had long since closed, and there were no other vehicles left in the hotel car park. I don't remember much of that night, accept the officer yelling out to the other officers when they released a couple of other inmates, "Leave Krone in there!"

The Dodge Truck

After an all-day drinking binge, which finished at the Southside Six Hotel, I was so drunk I saw double. I crashed through the intersection, taking out the front of a Volkswagen, then side-swiping a couple of other cars. I managed to drive home. Someone reported the incident and the next day the police called, and I had to go to the Waverley Police Station and make a statement. I was charged with dangerous driving, driving under the influence of alcohol and failing to stop at the scene of an accident. My solicitor got me off the drink driving and failing to stop. I didn't lose my licence and only had to pay $500.

Thank God for the Salvos

After my failed tree lopping and rubbish removal business, I started back on the Moorabbin Council as a Garbo and a second job, with the Reader family, who were Salvation Army officers, and had a contract with a butter factory to pick up the separated cream from various surrounding farms. They often encouraged me and prayed for me, giving many underserved opportunities.

One day after finishing my morning on the garbage trucks, I decided to have a few beers at the pub before I went to Braeside to start the cream run. I purchased half a dozen cans of UDL brandy lime and soda and headed off on the run. On this occasion, I was so drunk I don't remember most of that run. I vaguely remember going in and out of some farms along Coolart Road, Somerville.

Chapter 3   WORK, BOOZE & FAMILY

My boss Graham Reader was gracious to me even though I *hadn't* finished the run but *had* spilt cream all over the truck. He asked me to take the truck and clean it.

It would be another eight years before I would thank him sufficiently, sober, and a changed man. I went to see the Reader family and knocked on the door of the farm at about 7:00 pm. Graham answered the door, and I could see the dread and fear in his eyes when he realised it was me. I quickly reassured him I was a changed man and apologised for all my bad behaviour and thanked him and the family for their prayers to encourage them in their Christian faith. The greatest miracle is a changed life!

Paisley Court, Mulgrave

After turning 21, I received the compensation money from my accident that Dad had mentioned. We had an AV Jennings house built, which we moved into in the winter of 1970 before the completion of the estate's roads and footpaths. New houses didn't have gardens, concreted driveways, or paving up to the entry, and by the time the builders had finished, the front was a quagmire; we couldn't drive onto the property. We had to lay down old timber pallets and boards to get to the front porch and entrance on foot.

We had three kids under school age when we moved in. As I look back on the five years we were in our house in Mulgrave through Christian eyes, these times are ones of deep regret and missed opportunities to be a loving husband and father to my wife and fantastic kids.

Thank God for a loving mother who raised our kids on her own while I was away working, drinking, and partying. When I was at home, I usually put my wife and kids through the effects of my alcoholic lifestyle. Many years later, I learnt in Alcoholics Anonymous (alcoholism is a family disease) that the continual excessive abuse of alcohol has a profound effect on the rest of the family.

We'd paid about $12,000 for our new house in 1970, and in 1974, we'd put a $4000 extension on the rear of the property. We managed to sell in 1975 for $34,000.

Southampton

My married life was in shambles. Out of nine years of marriage, the last five had been on the edge of breaking point because of the broken promises, disloyalty, and unfaithfulness with my drunken behaviour. This included Jean waiting for me in various pub car parks with the kids to get some housekeeping money. Sometimes she had to get me from a police station or lie for me to keep me out of jail because of drunk driving. There was also a lack of moral support for her and the kids during this time. It had taken its toll on our marriage. By this stage, our family had grown considerably. Shane, our eldest, was now the big brother to Karen, Leanne, and little Brendan.

So, after five years in Mulgrave, we decided to sell up and go to England. Jean's family had migrated from England to Australia on the passenger ship *The Himalaya* in the early 1960s. They found Australia tough going and in the early 1970s decided to go back to England.

Going overseas for the first time was very exciting, as well as an opportunity for Jean to reunite with her family in England. It allowed me to leave behind all the problems that seem to be in my life. I remember having the self-image of a well-dressed jet-setter who was a fighting machine and was going on an overseas adventure. What a good bloke I was because I was taking my family on a working holiday.

After purchasing our tickets from British Airways and obtaining passports, there were many going away parties leading up to our departure from Tullamarine Airport on

Chapter 3   WORK, BOOZE & FAMILY

25th June 1975. We stored our furniture and left our car in Maurie's garage.

With the final farewells over and the excitement of our first flight taking off, it meant more partying for me, as the hostesses brought what seemed an endless supply of alcohol and food. We soon landed in Perth, Western Australia, to pick up more passengers for our flight to London.

We were forever grateful for one of the Perth passengers, as he was a specialist doctor from the Royal Children's Hospital in Perth. Once we had departed and were on our way, Brendan (our second son), started having trouble breathing. He also had a raging temperature. The cabin crew knew the doctor was on board, so they had him examine Brendan. He was alarmed and immediately administered medication and strongly suggested that his best chance of recovery would be to come down from the high altitude at our nearest airport, which was Singapore.

In 1975, Singapore, one of the drug capitals of the world, with a huge heroin epidemic. The main airport was annexed away from the city and was still operating as a third world airport. Passengers came down the steps of the plane onto the hot tarmac to collect their luggage and wait to catch a non-air-conditioned bus into the city, approximately 17 kilometres away.

British Airways were fantastic and arranged a doctor and further medication for Brendan and accommodation for me and Brendan as Jean, Shane, Karen, and Leanne travelled on to London. They also arranged for Jean to get the three kids through immigration, as they were on my Australian passport and not her British one.

Brendan started to get better as soon as we got down from the high altitude, and the medication kicked in. He was fascinated by the rickshaws, and the friendly Singaporeans seemed drawn to the cute four-year-old.

Eventually we arrived at Heathrow and were greeted by some of Jean's family, who took us by train to Southampton.

Through Jean's mum Mary, who was serving as a city councillor at the time, I was able to find employment as a conductor. I took fares on the cable drawn floating bridge that carried trucks, cars, motorbikes, bicycles and foot passengers across the Itchen River from Woolston to Southampton.

I loved my job on the ferry and was fascinated by the West Country accent. I felt at home with the working class and accepted when the locals referred to me as The Big Aussie Moosh. The term 'moosh' was an endearing slang term used by the locals in a comparable way to the Aussie slang greeting, 'G'day, mate.'

I was further amazed at their grammar. 'Ya right tharr, moosh?' 'Hey moosh, aye doos it do 'ey?' It sounded akin to hearing Long John Silver, the fearsome pirate. Some of the old mooshes wore an earring, not as a modern-day fashion statement, but as a legacy of the old seafaring days.

County Cricket Ground

My new lifestyle didn't last for long, my alcoholic lifestyle caught up with me, and the binge drinking started. I loved the English pubs, but I remember being annoyed that they called last orders at 2.00 pm and wouldn't reopen until 6.00 pm. On many occasions, rather than go home, I would purchase bottled beer and drink in the local park, usually with some 'paddies'. The Irishmen and the Aussies seemed to get along well, especially where alcohol was concerned.

The ferry job was shift work and involved weekends. I was rostered on to start in the afternoon for a 3.00 pm to 11.00 pm shift one Saturday. One day, I started drinking at the pub and went on a binge. I mainly drank lager, which was chilled, as opposed to the other English beers, which were served at room temperature and always in pint glasses. They were not as high in alcoholic content as Aussie beer, so I added a spirit chaser—brandy or whiskey.

I don't remember most of the afternoon, but vaguely remember turning up to the ferry late and drunk, argumentative and abusive. Work had to call in a relief conductor whom I wanted to fight. Eventually, someone called the police, just before I left the area. This was a blackout binge, and most of it was retold to me when I was called to stand before the corporation manager. I was dismissed from duty and lost my job.

I wasn't well educated and had no trade. I could drive trucks but only had an international licence so, I wasn't allowed to drive heavy or commercial vehicles in the UK. I applied for a job as a Garbo on the Southampton Council. About the only thing I had going for me was a work ethic. I only had a few other ethics in my life, but I was 27 years old, fit and strong, and was right in my element, showing the poms how we did it back in Australia.

We got a house on the old Southampton city side of the Itchen River. It was an old two-storey terrace house with no bathroom. It was temporary accommodation we had to stay in to qualify for a new council house.

The rickety old house was on the one-way traffic system that carried a lot of city traffic and commercial vehicles, including large trucks and trailers that rumbled past many times late at night, making the windows rattle. There was no insulation or double glazing, which meant it was freezing in winter and boiling in summer.

Apart from a wash in the kitchen sink, we had to walk a kilometre down to St Mary's Leisure Centre where we could have a hot shower. The old place had a coin-operated electric meter that would take 10 pence and 20 pence coins.

The Leisure Centre was not a family-friendly area, with many pimps, drug dealers, and undesirables loitering around, although there was a young couple with a baby who lived next door—John and Betty. They had some violent arguments. We could hear the crashing of items through the walls. We affectionately referred to her as f***ing Betty because every second word was the F-word; it didn't matter what company she was in.

Derby Road was opposite us, and on that corner was our local 'off-licence', the pommy version of a licensed grocer that also sold sweets, soft drink and ice cream. Derby Road was the home of the infamous red-light area of Southampton, where the girls would sit in the front windows. Directly opposite them was our local laundrette.

On one occasion while waiting for our laundry, one of the 'window girls' came running over in a panic, asking if someone could phone an ambulance as one of the customers, an older man, had had a massive heart attack after spending the last of his pension money.

***

The euphoria and excitement of living in England soon wore off. Since working as a garbo again, I had found a new lot of drinking mates, so I would be off binge drinking, eventually crawling home like a mangy dog.

Many times, I felt remorse at causing fear and guilt so I would plead, 'just give me another chance', but it was more lies and broken promises that caused our marriage to become unbearable.

I thought it might help if we all went on a holiday to Western Europe. This was another of my 'geographicals'; a term used in Alcoholics Anonymous, where an alcoholic will try and move to another location, believing they will leave their problems behind.

Chapter 3 WORK, BOOZE & FAMILY

We hired a VW campervan and headed across the English Channel from Southampton to Le Havre, then travelled up the Normandy coast to Belgium.

After settling into our first campsite somewhere near the area of Waterloo, the kids wanted to run and play with the other kids in the van park. We knew the FA Cup final was on and heard on Radio Luxembourg that Southampton had defeated Manchester United 1–0 thanks to a goal in the 83rd minute from Bobby Stokes.

The same evening, we phoned Jean's parents, who had heard the news that Councillor Mary Key was elected the next Mayor of Southampton.

We had a wonderful time together as a family. The kids had a great time. They particularly loved Salzburg, Austria, where we camped on the lush, pristine banks of the beautiful Salzach River with its bright azure crystal clear water. We felt as though we were a part of *The Sound of Music*, as we were at some of the locations where the movie was filmed.

The sixth of May 1976 was a beautiful late spring evening at a campsite in Switzerland when we all felt the Earth move. It went on for about a minute. We figured it must have been an earthquake.

It wasn't until later that we heard on Radio Luxembourg there had been a bad earthquake in Italy on the other side of the Alps. It was the Friuli Earthquake, with a magnitude of 6.5, leaving 978 dead and 2400 injured.

The morning after the earthquake, as we left our campsite, I had a brain fade more than likely caused by the many Swiss beers consumed the night before and drove onto the left-hand side of the road.

In the last second, before colliding with oncoming vehicles, I wrenched the steering wheel to get us on the correct side. As I think back on this, I realise how close I'd come to death and destruction. I truly believe the hand of

God Almighty protected my family and even me, the self-proclaimed atheist.

We were on the outskirts of Paris and heading to Le Havre to catch our ferry back to England and needed fuel I couldn't speak French and simply looked at the different petrol bowsers and pointed to the one that had the cheapest price, the driveway attendant was saying No! No! He was pointing to the other more expensive bowser, so in my ignorance and arrogance insisted on the cheapest one so he filled the VW camper-van up with (fuel oil) basically (2 stroke mower fuel). After paying, and driving away, my thoughts were that I had outsmarted this Frog and drove out onto the Autobahn/motorway, but we didn't get too far before the motor overheated and blew up.

The Gendarmes could speak English and were very helpful; first asking if the family were ok, and then organising the emergency breakdown truck to tow us to the nearest French village. It was Pacy-Sur-Eure in the Normandy region of North West France. It was a small village with a population of around 3500, we found the folk very friendly and helpful. They looked after Jean and the kids and organised for me to notify the car hire company back in England, that their vehicle had broken down, and for transport into Paris to get money transferred from our bank in London.

The local post office was where a doctor and his wife had heard of my need and offered to take me into Paris as his surgery was there. It was an old Renault two-door with a soft top, his wife, a blonde lady, sat beside him in the front, and I was in the back with their large hairy dog. We travelled about 20 kilometres weaving in and out of traffic at a frenetic pace.

We stopped at a large motorway petrol station. The doctor spoke to one of the attendants, and within a couple of minutes the car was being jacked up like a race car at a pit stop. The attendants removed the wheels to replace the tyres. I couldn't help but notice the old tyres were worn down to the canvas! The rest of the journey into Paris was just as hair-raising, but a least we now had good tyres. The doctor was in a lather of sweat by the time we got into central Paris.

But the *piece de resistance* of his driving skill was in front of his surgery. By the time he'd finished parking, after bashing and crashing, the old Renault had its front bumper up on the bumper bar of the car in front. This time I was very sober, and while being grateful, will never forget the tyres being worn down to the canvas, the frenetic driving, and the creative parking.

***

After the holidays, life continued as *normal,* with the addition that Jean's Mum had been promoted to 'Mr Mayor' (it even sounded sexist back in 1976).

During a time of great celebration in England as the victorious 'Saints' Southampton football team, had held high the FA Cup, after defeating Manchester United at Wembley Stadium. Celebrations for most had died off after a week or so, and *most* of Southampton got on with their lives; but I was in party mode still, and my selfish life was only satisfied with alcohol. My delusional thoughts when drunk was that I was God's gift to women. My life and morals were disgusting, as were the words that came out of my mouth. At this stage of my life, it didn't matter if I broke all the rules, as long as I didn't get caught. After all, I was an atheist.

I had started working as a garbo on Southampton Council and got along well with most of the blokes. Jock and Yorkie were two who became my regular drinking mates. One night we had arranged to meet at the pub near their boarding house after we had finished our garbage rounds.

It was Friday and, after 'getting the taste', we wanted to keep drinking. After the pub closed at 2.00 pm, we armed ourselves with bottled beer and spirits and drove all around Southampton until the pubs re-opened again at 6.00 pm. Then we did a pub crawl until closing time at 11.00 pm.

It was about 2.00 am Saturday when I decided to pull over to have a sleep. Jock and Yorkie were blind drunk and asleep on the back seat. I was so drunk, I was seeing double and had one eye closed while I was driving.

Outside the county cricket ground in Southampton, I steered over onto the guttering. The trouble was, as I kept driving forward, the guttering went up on an angle. By the time I came to a stop, the car was on a precarious 45-degree angle.

I turned the ignition off and fell asleep. I don't know how long it was until Mr Plod drove past and noticed, but I was arrested and taken to the Southampton Police Station.

While they didn't catch me drink driving, the keys were in the ignition, and I was charged with being drunk in charge of a motor vehicle. Jock and Yorkie had to walk home after the police helped them out of the car.

I was released and went home later that day after the police informed Jean that I had been arrested. She came down to the police station early Saturday morning to pick up this drunk who was supposed to be a husband and father.

Where was God in All This?

My family weren't practising Christians; I think Mum and Dad may have gone to church a couple of times. As a kid, I remember thinking that God was there, or maybe it was grandmother, who had lived with us and died in the early 1960s, watching over me. But I clearly remember as an adult deciding that I was an atheist. My feelings following that time seemed euphoric; I guess I liked my

new-found freedom to do whatever I liked with few or no consequences.

But as I think back, I thank God no one was injured or killed because of my selfish actions. I may not have believed in Him, but He believed and cared for me, even though my life looked like it did. The Bible says, "*But God demonstrates His own love toward us, sending His son to die for us and not waiting until we had everything worked out to offer salvation. (Rom. 5:8)*

As you read on, you'll see that I had a long way to go before I saw God, but I do know now that God saw me! If your journey now is anything like you're reading, know that God wants you to know that regardless of whatever you've done, or what has happened to you, you'll never be beyond His Love which is full of mercy and grace.

Chapter 4

THE ROAD TO HELL

We departed Heathrow on the fourth of July 1976, and our family headed back to Australia. Right up until a few days before our departure, I wasn't sure if Jean and the kids wanted to come back with me. Again, I thought we'd get away from all the problems. 'It must be England and the poms.' I still believed I didn't have a drinking problem, just a bit of bad luck. Things would be much better back in Australia.

We enrolled the kids at Rye Primary School, and all these Krones in the same school was a shock for the teachers. The 'pommy' kids in England had given them a tough time for having weird accents, so they soon sounded like little poms. Now back in Australia, they copped it for having pommy accents and had to change again!

We stayed with Mum and Dad at Rye. They'd retired, as Dad was not in good health and was diagnosed with kidney disease. He also suffered from angina and chronic gout, as well as a hiatus hernia. He had been working for WC Stevens Pty Ltd as a fitter. They produced exhaust systems for the motor industry.

Mum had been employed by the Reserve Bank of Australia, counting the old paper notes before being destroyed. It was a job she loved, but Dad and his needs were more important, so they sold their house in East Bentleigh and moved to Rye. This was a great tonic for Dad, and together, they had transformed their holiday house into their permanent home.

They grew their own vegetables, herbs and fruit trees with flathead tails being a key part of their diet too, as they were involved at the Rye fishing club.

***

The next five years, I was unwittingly headed down a dark, destructive path as there was no God and no spiritual realm, certainly none of this nonsense about the devil or Satan. I was like a lot of my Aussie mates— if you can't see it, it isn't there!'

We'd managed to leave enough money back in Australia for a deposit on a house that we purchased in Blairgowrie. With a bank loan, we bought a truck on contract at Hillview Quarry. We also bought a new 1976 HQ Holden and modern furniture, so the mortgage was maxed out.

I was building for myself a very nice false self-image that I was successful. I was providing for my wife and family the material things needed but not the love and support of a husband and father which was really needed. Life, in a nutshell, was all about me. I was full of pride, ignorance and arrogance.

I became a committee member of the Rye Football Club, which was more of a self-exalted status rather than helping the club and community. With my years of pub experience, I soon volunteered to run the Sunday beer barrel that sold beer to raise money for the club. I always gravitated to an activity or event where there was alcohol. Through this, I found another way to justify my being away from home because, in my mind, this was a significant role, more so than being a father and husband.

This continued lifestyle had a compounding effect on our marriage and was eventually too much to bear for my

Chapter 4   THE ROAD TO HELL

wife and kids. They moved away from me for their self-preservation and sanity. At the time, I should've been more devastated. But having lived in the UK and now back home, I found solace by connecting with some single blokes who had also spent some time in the UK, that I thought were 'living the dream'. We would have a good laugh, and often shared stories of some of our drunken behaviour at pubs and parties while in the UK.

The Adventures of Barry McKenzie and *Barry McKenzie Holds His Own,* were two movies starring Barry Crocker that came out in the early to mid-1970s. They told the story of an Australian 'yobbo' travelling through the United Kingdom. These movies were symbolic of the Aussie expat life in London.

I thought they were fantastic. This lifestyle was what it was all about, things like snakebite pints at 10 in the morning, AFL grand finals with your mates, drunken hook-ups with girls, with all the crude vulgarity of the Aussie and Kiwi sub-culture. I immersed myself in this sub-culture, living the life of a single man, and life became one big party.

Eventually, like all parties, it came to an end with a sudden jolt of reality and a downward spiral left me at a low point but still not rock bottom yet. I sold the family home and the truck to pay the debt and was broke. It was around this time I had a breakdown and ended up in the hospital.

I had gone back to stay with my parents. One day I had chest pains and a panic attack. I thought I was dying and said to Mum and Dad, 'Tell Jean and the kids I love them!' Dad thought I was having a heart attack and gave me one of his angina tablets to put under my tongue until the ambulance arrived.

Dad was very ill by then, and as I think back, waves of shame came over me because of the way I treated a dad who loved me and only wanted the best for me. He had witnessed

15 years of my alcoholic lifestyle and had seen his son turn into a monster.

Two events with Dad still haunt me today and have left me with the scars of deep regret. The first was at my 21st birthday party.

Mum and Dad opened their home and catered for family and our friends. It was a great night until the effects of excessive alcohol started to change my personality, as it always did. (Scientists have discovered that alcohol abuse can cause tremendous changes to your personality. Normal personality traits can disappear during intoxication and be taken over by selfish, angry and egotistical behaviour. Aggression and mood swings are common, as well as a general deterioration of morals.)

Early on Sunday morning, when the beer had run out, I went off at him in a drunken rage, accusing him of hiding it. Dad wasn't an aggressive person, although he could look after himself—he was trained in self-defence—but he never reacted to my aggression. My parents never gave me any corporal punishment because of the accident I'd had as a baby. They thought the drunken rants and negative behaviour were perhaps a result of the car accident, leaving me with slight brain damage.

On the second occasion, while Mum was giving Dad palliative care at home, he questioned me about some trivial thing, and I lost my temper and shouted at him. I will never forget Mum trying to make me calm down with a serious, hushed tone, 'Don't do it. Your dad is dying!'

Lysaght's

John Lysaght (Australia) Pty Ltd was founded in 1918. They had started production at Westernport Hastings in the early 1970s. I had no idea how significant working at Lysaght

Steel Westernport and being in Hastings would become in the latter part of my life.

Through the assistance of a decent bloke named John L Roberts, well known in the recycling industry, who happened to know the manager of the Organic Fishing Department for John Lysaght Western at Port Hastings.

He needed an operator and instructed the personnel manager to take me through an induction course. I started on C crew as the finish operator on the number three paint line.

At this time, I had moved back in with Jean and the kids, and we were renting a house at Karingal. Why she took me back I'll never know, but it was good timing as unknown to us at the time, Mum and Dad's time together was coming to an end. They had three years in their retirement house. Mum and Dad had a good marriage. They loved each other and were best friends. Mum shared with me that in their last meeting before he died, he held her hand told her that he loved her and had no regrets! Unfortunately, my marriage was not reflecting theirs.

I'll never forget that fateful day when my eldest son Shane, who was 13 at the time, came running out the back, panic-stricken, to tell us it was his Nan on the phone with the news we were dreading—that Grandpa had died. It was early November 1979, just after his 65th birthday.

My younger brother Ross at this time, was at Ararat Prison, located about 200 kilometres west of Melbourne, serving time for armed robbery. He was a heroin addict and had tried to hold up a chemist in the inner Melbourne suburb of Malvern. Ross was not a violent person but had been desperate for a fix and had walked into the chemist with an unloaded shotgun and said, 'I want some drugs!' The chemist replied, 'You're the third one this week. We haven't got any.' Ross said, 'Okay.' Then he turned around and walked out. He hadn't tried to hide his identity and was later arrested.

Ross had been in and out of different prisons around Australia on drug-related and petty criminal activity and had learnt to survive in horrific circumstances. In was only the month before, that I had done something really good for my Dad and brother (a rare a thing at the time), when I drove Dad to Ararat Prison, not realising at the time that it would be the last time they'd see each other this side of eternity. It would've destroyed Ross if he hadn't seen him before he died.

It was my shift's weekend off from the paint line. Mum had asked if I could go back up to Ararat Prison, as they would release Ross into my custody to attend Dad's funeral.

Because of his war service, Dad, who had been classified as totally and permanently incapacitated, qualified for a military funeral service with the Australian flag over his coffin, provided by their local Rye RSL. I don't remember much of the service, but I do remember having a gut full of grog, which gave me enough courage to steel myself so that I wouldn't shed a tear at his funeral.

My parents never spoke about death to us as kids or discussed what happened after you die. They'd generally avoided the issue and, like many, 'whistled when walking past the graveyards of life'. We had never even been to a funeral. The only other family member I knew that had died was Nanna Krone, and we were told, 'Nanna's gone to heaven', and we didn't get to go to her funeral.

The wake was at the Rye RSL was another blackout session for me. I vaguely even remember driving Ross back to Ararat Prison and being so drunk I had double vision, having to close one eye to stay on the road. It was a six-hour round trip, and I believe God sent angels to protect me, my brother and other unsuspecting motorists.

Chapter 4   THE ROAD TO HELL

With the combined events of the last three years, I was now at a place of total brokenness. I was physically, mentally, and spiritually bankrupt after my father's death, and, for the *final* time, I separated from my wife and family.

My drinking increased, and my health worsened to the point that I couldn't cope with the pressure of rotating shift work and applied for day work at Lysaght's as a trade's assistant. I was grossly overweight and sick with ulcers and gout. I had borrowed money from friends and family that I couldn't pay back, as well as money owed to the local licenced grocer, and utility bills overdue. I was desperate and felt I had no one to cry out to. Even my Dad was gone!

I considered myself fully atheist. I thought at the time that this gave me the freedom to do whatever I wanted as long as I didn't get caught. I believed there was no God to answer to when I died, as there was nothing there. I enjoyed the demise of Christians I knew, and thought Christianity was irrelevant, and I particularly enjoyed demoralising Ray, who had dared to try and share about his faith and belief in the Bible with me.

Looking back, I realise that it was not the freedom I was living in and the death of my Father made me realise that I had no hope! No hope for the next day, no hope that life would be better tomorrow. No meaning to life except whatever it took for the next drink.

Now, as I'm writing this, I do have hope; including great hope that I will see Dad in heaven. My understanding is that he desperately wanted to go on living, and before he died, he called for faith healing and that a Salvation Army officer prayed with him.

I have this hope based on two things. First, it's God's heart that none should perish. Jesus' words are eternal and true when He said, "For God loved the world so much that

He gave his one and only Son so that everyone who believes in him will not perish but have eternal life." (John 3:16)

Second, God Almighty knows the thoughts and intentions of every human being and whether they would exercise their faith and believe in Jesus Christ to be their saviour. I believe that God's grace extends to every person right up until the actual point of death.

> Luke 23: 39-43 tells us that Jesus while on the cross, extended this same hope to one of the criminals hanging beside him when he asked, "Jesus, remember me when you come into your Kingdom." And Jesus replied, "I assure you, today you will be with me in paradise."

This hope is available to each and every one of us, including me! My Mum knew this about me. Regardless of all the behaviour, she was witnessing. She had hope, birthed many years ago on another fateful day.

Chapter 5

THE ROAD TO FREEDOM

Alone and separated, I felt empty and abandoned. I had let not only my wife and kids down but the rest of the family, including Mum. I had alienated anyone who had been with me while I was drinking because of my drunken violent, obnoxious behaviour. I was alone and felt consumed with dread, fear, and the pain of emptiness and failure.

The voice inside my head was becoming incessantly loud and clear, 'Just put the gun in your mouth and squeeze the trigger and you will be out of it.' If life looked like this, why did I still have such desperation to live? Something inside of me was crying out that there was more. I wrestled with suicidal thoughts, believing that perhaps that was all I had left. Silently screaming out to a God I didn't believe existed. At first, I felt nothing, I even managed to get some sleep, but the next morning.

I woke up as I usually did, with the dry horrors, but instead of reaching for the 'hair of the dog', I rang Bill.

Bill was the primary coat operator on the paint line, located above me in the finish coat room at Lysaght's Hastings. He eventually became a friend. He seemed to understand my lifestyle and could relate to where I was at, at that time.

Bill, a bricklayer by trade, had decided on a career change. He had formally been a chronic alcoholic who had hit rock bottom and found his way to Alcoholics Anonymous.

He went through the 12-step program and, after maintaining sobriety for a few years, so the fog of his mind cleared, he began to learn what step 11 of AA was about—'We sought through prayer and meditation to improve our conscious contact with God, praying only for knowledge of His will for us and the power to carry it out.'

In his quest to find the truth, Bill studied AA's *Big Book*, written by Dr Robert Smith (known as Dr Bob) and Bill Wilson (known as Bill W). They were the two recovering alcoholics who founded AA in 1935. They found that they, too, had a spiritual experience with the God of Christianity, strongly influenced by the Oxford Group, a Christian fellowship founded by American Christian missionary, Dr Franklin Buchman.

Bill befriended me and spent many of our days off with me, beach fishing, or fishing off the rocks. He was right into it, using the best casting drum reels and a good selection of rods. He checked the tides and wind direction and knew what bait to use.

Bill didn't talk about God or Christianity to me, but on one occasion, he said that if I ever needed any help with alcohol or related problems to ring and let him know. I immediately got my back up and let him have it. 'I'm not an alcoholic, you idiot!' It unnerved me that Bill didn't drink or smoke, so I told him that he would die a lonely old man because He would outlive all his friends! But, a seed had been planted.

After phoning Bill feeling embarrassed, I reminded him of his offer to help me with my problems. He immediately arranged to take me to Alcoholics Anonymous meetings. The AA process is known as '12 stepping'. There were meetings all over Melbourne every evening and many day meetings too.

I was encouraged just to sit and listen and was amazed to realise that alcoholism respects no one. People from all

Chapter 5 THE ROAD TO FREEDOM

walks of life, both young and old, were affected by the disease. I had thought an alcoholic was one of those blokes who was homeless and lived in the park or on the street, so I was surprised to hear the testimony of young professional businessmen and women, high court judges, doctors, CEOs of large corporations, blue-collar workers, and many of the working class.

Maybe I did have a problem! Up until that point, I thought that while I had some problems, I was not an alcoholic. That is the insanity of the disease.

The first month was difficult as I fought off the physical craving for alcohol, but I was encouraged by some of the speakers at the meetings who had kept going by sticking at it and putting the 12 steps into practice. Some shared how they had relapsed and had that first drink, which set them right back to rock bottom. It's believed in AA that alcoholism is a progressive disease and that there is no going back.

I remember 'Antique Harry', as he was known, in line with AA members' anonymity, but what he shared had a lasting impact on my life. As a young man, he had become a chronic alcoholic and found his way to an AA meeting. After achieving a period of sobriety, he slowly stopped attending meetings, felt good and got involved in business, eventually owning a string of antique shops. He maintained sobriety for 20 years until after having great financial success, he thought he'd take up the offer of going out to a bar to have just one drink to celebrate. He lost everything he had; in fact, his alcoholism took him to a lower place than he had been before, to the point of drinking pure alcohol that was used in antique furniture restoration. Antique Harry quoted a couple of the many clichés used in AA, 'One drink is too many, and a thousand is not enough' and 'When Daniel got out of the lion's den he didn't go back down for his hat!'

Bill Magher stuck with me over the next three months, taking me to many AA meetings, but as it turned out, he had some good news he was bursting to share, which was far greater than being sober, as good as it was.

When he felt the timing was right, he explained how he had become a born-again Christian and experienced God's love and forgiveness (John 3:3–16). He didn't use religious words out of the bible, and in hindsight, I don't think I would have been ready for that. He spoke to me in a way I could understand. He had my ear, being a knockabout Aussie bloke. He wasn't perfect, but open and honest, and I knew he was fair dinkum when he shared how he had sensed the tangible presence of God and could speak in a heavenly language.

He tried to explain how his God encounter had felt for him in a way he thought I would understand, so he said, 'It was an amazing experience, better than having sex.' That got my attention. I asked if he could take me with him to experience the feeling too! Bill took me to Dandenong Assemblies of God Church with him the following Sunday night. They were hiring the town hall to hold their meetings.

Evangelist Tim Hall who had moved from South Australia to Victoria was the main speaker. After the happy clapping and 'hallelujahs', part of the meeting. He preached a gospel message to a packed-out Sunday night meeting. It was January 1983. Tim shared some personal stories of his own. He held such confidence that God was very real and interested in my life, but sin that is in every person separates us from the grace that God longs to offer. He said, 'all of us are sinners, and the penalty for sin is death with eternal separation from God. By ourselves, we are helpless to be able to do anything about it.'

I had no problem accepting that truth for myself; I was certainly a sinner – I knew what I had done was wrong; there was so much wrong. Tim's confidence that there is a God challenged my own now seriously waning atheist belief.

Chapter 5   THE ROAD TO FREEDOM

What if he was right? What if there was a God? And then what of this sin of mine? What could I possibly do to make things right?

Turns, out that there was only one thing to do. Tim described one simple step, one simple decision. I needed a saviour, and I needed Him to be Lord over my life. Alcohol had lorded over my life for so long. My heart cried forgiveness, healing and freedom. According to what Tim was saying, Jesus Christ could offer this. He asked for those who were interested to raise their hand. I raised my hand, along with many others.

Tim said, 'I see your hand' to each person who responded, then after the band had played another song, he asked those of us who had raised our hands to come forward.

When I stood up to go forward, Bill explained later he was shocked and excited at the same time because he hadn't seen me raise my hand. I don't remember anything much of what Tim said during the meeting. My thoughts were still on what Bill had said about his wonderful feeling when he'd encountered God. I wanted it too, so I went forward without any other understanding, simply a desire to meet God and get that wonderful feeling.

Walking down the front, I felt embarrassed and uncomfortable that all these people were watching me. It was certainly not what Bill had described. I had stepped out of my comfort zone with no alcohol to give me the courage I usually had. It was all me – facing God who knew everything about me, EVERYTHING!

Tim asked if he could pray for us and told me how I could invite Jesus to be Lord of my life. That moment changed the trajectory of my life forever. I would never be the same. Life would never be the same. At that moment I walked *off* the road to hell and never looked back

It amazes me that God was there the whole time. In hindsight, I see how persistent He was in looking for me, but I just kept looking the other way. How many people before Bill had tried to share either by word or action that God is real? He had a greater plan for me than I did for myself.

In that moment of desperation, where I exercised the tiniest piece of faith that perhaps there is a God. In an instant, His grace allowed me to turn from being an atheist to at least an agnostic, open to God. God was somewhere out there! God heard my SOS and sent me Bill and then Tim. It truly was Amazing Grace!

I was so much like Jonah in the Bible, who had ignored God and ran away from Him. He found himself in a place that was hell on earth, no possible way of moving forward, — stuck in a deep dark prison of his own doing. I thought Atheism and doing whatever I wanted was freedom.

But it was a prison. I had managed to stay out of jail legally, but I was a prisoner and slave to self and alcohol.

I was almost convinced suicide would end the pain. Jonah jumped ship to save those on board. I thought my suicide might be the answer to the pain I felt and the pain I had caused so many others, in particular, my family.

But God rescued Jonah, from the depths of hades, and He rescued me! So, I can relate to Jonah's desperate prayer from inside the big fish!

> *Then Jonah prayed to the Lord his God from the fish's belly. And he said: "I cried out to the Lord because of my affliction...the waters surrounded me, even to my soul; The deep closed around me; Weeds were wrapped around my head. I went down to the moorings of the mountains; The earth with its bars closed behind me forever;*

Chapter 5 THE ROAD TO FREEDOM

Yet You have brought up my life from the pit, O Lord, my God."

(Jonah 2:1–6 NKJV)

Are you a prisoner of alcohol or anything else? Do you feel like you're in hell, possibly even a hell of your making? Your way of doing things may have seemed ok at first, as it certainly did for me. I had started just having fun, doing whatever felt good with no thought of anyone else, just my selfish desires. I realise now that while I did have free will, all of us have. I was ripped off, unwittingly being led down a pathway of self-destruction by a deceptive enemy that I didn't even believe existed. But now my spiritual eyes were opened to the truth, having received God's amazing love. I was saved literally. Jesus Christ became my Saviour. My message to you is that God Almighty loves you regardless of the circumstances you are in right now, or of the events of your past life.

The thief's purpose is to steal and kill and destroy. My purpose is to give (YOU) ... a rich and satisfying life. John 10:10. Whether you believe it or not, there is a real enemy that wants nothing else but for you to be lost in your own will, desire, and destruction. God purposes in another way. Which way would you choose?

Chapter 6

NEW BEGINNINGS

I hadn't seen Bill for some time, and while I had stayed sober, there hadn't been any follow up in my new Christian faith. I had gone back onto shift work at Lysaght's and had met a wonderful lady named Lindy.

I first met Lindy at a social night dance which was, interestingly, at a local pub. I had been sober for about three months and amazingly wasn't there for the alcohol. My life was slowly changing. Lindy has never been a drinker but was at that time struggling with self-confidence after going through an acrimonious divorce.

From the very beginning, we were open and honest with each other about our previous lives and enjoyed being together. We began a romance and after falling in love, decided to move in together.

During the next year, we both began to explore what living out Christian faith was. It was during this time that Lindy too made her own decision, as she too recognised her own desperate need for a saviour. We grew together both in our faith and relationship with Jesus Christ and for each other.

Together we faced the many blessings and challenges that a blended family can bring. I have four children, and she has two. Two different family grounds coming together and with both of us so new in the faith, we didn't always get it right, but we recognised that we were no longer doing it on our own. We had God, and we were so thankful for His grace because we needed it! We loved our kids, we loved each other, and we loved Jesus and wanted God's blessing on our lives, so we decided to get married.

We had little money and couldn't afford a wedding venue, so the ceremony was held in the backyard of our home. Friends and blended family came together; we enjoyed a great day.

The chaplain from John Lysaght's agreed to marry us and had asked before the marriage, 'What type of ceremony do you want?' 'We want a full-on Christian spirit-filled marriage ceremony!' I was over the top with my understanding of spirit-filled Christianity. I certainly wasn't exercising wisdom or sensitivity. As always hindsight teaches us these things, but I had made so many bad decisions in the past with both alcohol and self, having been the previous lord over my life and for so long, that I was passionate about Jesus being the new Lord over my life and I wanted everyone to know it and experience what I had. I just wanted to get it right. I hadn't learnt yet, that grace comes in all sizes; that it's certainly not 'one size fits all'.

Thankfully, the chaplain was a warm, friendly bloke, not judgemental and religious, but a wise, effective, spirit-filled Christian with years of experience. He could talk to you on whatever your level. He had great discernment and didn't discourage me in my zeal for the Lord. He became a role model for me because of the way he went about being a Christian minister and demonstrating grace.

It would be many years later, that I would one day work as a marriage celebrant, with many opportunities to explain to couples during the premarital talk of how Lindy and I have a great marriage *because*, right from the start, we made a choice to have God in our marriage. I tell them how we received God's gift of salvation and forgiveness through

Chapter 6 NEW BEGINNINGS

the amazing grace of Jesus Christ even though our previous lives had become a broken, hurtful mess.

There was a wonderful moment during our wedding ceremony. When the chaplain read some scripture and was praying for us, the sun broke through the clouds. For Lindy and me, there was an overwhelming feeling of God's love toward us as we expressed our love for each other on our special day. I could sense the tangible presence of the Holy Spirit as tears came to my eyes. For me, it was an affirmation of God's full blessing on our marriage.

It was a new beginning for us. The challenges of life were still there, and I knew I had so much to make up for in the life of my kids, but it was different this time. I didn't have to face the battles alone. I thank God for sending Lindy to walk the journey with me, but most of all, I thank God, that I had Him to walk the journey with me. When we recognise Jesus as Lord of our life, it frees us from having to have all the answers all the time.

Proverbs 3:5-6 says, "Trust in the Lord with all your heart and lean not on your own understanding. In all your ways submit to Him, and He will make your paths straight".

With faith, I had God in my life, and because Lindy shared this faith, we had God in our marriage too. We're weren't perfect and never will be, but we had God from which to seek understanding and courage. Alcohol no longer had the pull it had had over me for so long. I had a future and a hope of new beginnings and knowing I was never alone!

Chapter 7

DOUBTS AT THE RIVER JORDAN

I had been at an evening service at the Dandenong Town Hall similar to the meeting where I was 'saved', when a visiting speaker said he was hosting a tour of Israel for believers from various churches around Melbourne. He went on and shared about some of the things and experiences that would be on tour. Once again, Bill, who had been so instrumental in my life, was with me. We were both so excited about what we heard, that he said, 'Let's put our names down!' We were both caught up in the excitement and hadn't thought if our wives would be okay with it, let alone the cost. I had no money and was still paying off debt, and I think Bill was in a similar financial position.

Lindy had been gracious enough to let me go, considering we had only been married for six months and had to use the bank card credit to finance the tour, then pay it back when I returned on the strength of my new job at Frankston TAFE. It was so exciting when we were finally on our way to Israel, after all the pre-tour meetings.

Athens was our first stopover, where we got to see the many ancient ruins and monuments like the Acropolis, Parthenon, the Temple of Hephaestus, and many others. But our focus was on the places mentioned in the bible, particularly Areopagus on Mars Hill, where the Apostle Paul spoke to the Athenians. We had a time of prayer and read out the scripture from Acts 17:16–34.

The next day we travelled by coach along the coast to the ruins of ancient Corinth, crossing over the Corinth Canal, which connects the Gulf of Corinth with the Saronic Gulf in the Aegean Sea. It cuts through the narrow Isthmus of Corinth and separates the Peloponnese from the Greek mainland.

One of the points of interest to us, since Israel was our focus, was that Emperor Nero had used 6,000 Jewish prisoners of war to start digging the canal out in CE 67. We were reminded that this was once a heavily populated city in the Roman Empire, notorious for sexual immorality, as we walked up and down the streets of the Corinthian ruins.. In those days, to slander someone, they would accuse them of acting 'like a Corinthian'.

It's to this backdrop that the Apostle Paul often wrote in his letters about the grace that he had received that was freely available to both the Jews and the Gentiles, regardless of their sinful lifestyles.

Saul/Paul had been opposed to Christianity, trying to have as many Christians killed as possible with the sincere belief that he was doing it for God, that is until he encountered God and received the truth on the road to Damascus. (Acts 9:3-6).

God is personal, and Paul's encounter was personal, and it changed his lifestyle forever! He became one of Christ's greatest defenders as he embraced the truth that God loved *all* humanity, even though *all* have sinned. That, yes, the penalty for sin is death—eternal separation from God and His Heaven. But in His profound love, God gave us a priceless gift we didn't deserve by paying the price for our sin through the sacrifice of His only begotten Son. Jesus said, "*I am the way, the truth, and the life.* No one *can come to the Father except through me."* [Emphasis added] (John 14:6)

Chapter 7 DOUBTS AT THE RIVER JORDAN

No one can earn enough Brownie points ever to reach heaven, regardless of how good we will ever be. It is only by His grace!

Jesus Christ is *the* personification of GRACE; He gave up His life to pay our debt of sin – His gift to us. Because of the finished work of the cross, Christ's death, burial and resurrection have fulfilled every legal requirement in heaven's courtroom. Justice has been served, the ransom price has been paid, and the anger of a holy, righteous God appeased. It was a sealed deal when Jesus uttered his last words on the cross 'It is finished!' John 19:30

Dick, who was leading our tour, seemed to know the bible well and was zealous in his love for the Jewish people. His first few talks were friendly and informative, particularly with his understanding of the Old Testament. But after arriving in Israel, whenever we had a chance for a chat or when he spoke to us as a group, he seemed to me to become Old Testament-focused. Being a new Christian, I hadn't learnt a lot of the bible.

On one occasion, he said to me words that shocked and challenged me as a new Christian. 'God hates divorce, Vic, and sinful wrongdoing is no excuse for divorce. In God's eyes, you're still married to your first wife!' Doubts came to my mind. *Am I really saved? What about my marriage to Lindy? What about my first wife's marriage to her new husband?* How can I possibly measure up?

Dick had been raised in a bible-believing family in the Open Brethren Church and knew the bible well, especially the Old Testament scriptures when God was speaking to the nation of Israel. His love for the Jewish people was taught to him by his Dutch parents who, during World War II, were in the Dutch underground of Nazi-occupied Holland. For years they jeopardised their lives by hiding a Jewish man in a wall cavity in their home.

He shared how his father was disturbed with the brutal and senseless murder of almost all of Europe's Jews. Holland and other nations lost up to 98% of their Jewish communities. He also told us that in 1947, two men from the Brethren Church startled his father by insisting that the Jewish people were still in covenant relationship with God. They revealed to him from the bible that God fully intended to bring the Jews back to their land and back to himself.

After studying the relevant scriptures, he realised his previous understanding that the Jews had rejected Jesus and, in turn, God had rejected them and replaced them with the Church was wrong. Dick's belief about marriage, was based on God's relationship with Israel. He believes that Israel's sins in the Old Testament could in no way dissolve the covenant between God and Israel. Therefore, he believed that the covenant of Christian marriage cannot be broken because of sin, even adultery.

As a new Christian, all I knew was I had been sin-sick physically, mentally, and spiritually, locked in a prison with invisible bars and a slave to my selfish alcoholic lifestyle for 18 years. It had robbed me of my marriage and family life, and I despaired of life itself. But God had heard my cry for help, and I found salvation, healing, freedom and destiny. I found God's love through His amazing grace. I didn't know how to truly love until I met Jesus.

I was newly married and madly in love with Lindy, my soulmate and best friend, and was so excited and eager to know more about my Saviour, Jesus, and to walk where he walked in Israel 2000 years ago. Dick's words were not spoken to be malicious, but from a man who was sincere in his understanding of God's word and his love for God's chosen people, the Jews. For me, it was the first major test of my new Christian faith.

But God was there and met me in that very place, He gave me comfort and reassurance, and I believe He reminded me

Chapter 7 DOUBTS AT THE RIVER JORDAN

of our wedding day, when I had sensed the tangible presence of the Holy Spirit, and my eyes filled with tears.

Other strong Christians on the tour who heard Dick's teaching about marriage came alongside me and said they thought he was out of line, especially to me, a new Christian. One couple, in particular, Rodney and Irene Stevens, spirit-filled Salvation Army officers, stuck with me for the rest of the tour, and we stayed in touch even after returning home.

It was a lesson that in all things, we must go back to God and what the Bible says rather than people's opinion. With encouragement from Rodney and Irene Stevens, the Salvo officers, I enjoyed the rest of the tour. This experience brought me closer to the Lord, and I prayed more often.

Our kibbutz accommodation around Israel was fantastic with good healthy food. Most kibbutz had a swimming pool, which we were glad of, as it was so hot.

We had lots of laughs and special moments. We arrived at our kibbutz at Bethany near the Jordan River. It was an area often used by visitors to Israel who wanted to be baptised. There were quite a few of us on the tour baptised the following day. I decided there, just as Jesus was baptised, that I also wanted to be baptised in the water. It was explained to me, that I hadn't been saved by water baptism, but it was an external demonstration of what happened internally when I prayed the sinner's prayer, and that I was doing it in obedience to Christ Jesus.

Our group had to wait for the large crowd to come back up the concrete ramp, after being baptised in the Jordan River. Dr Robert Schuller was leading them. At its peak, his Californian Orange County-based ministry operated the Crystal Cathedral in Garden Grove. His *Hour of Power* television program put Schuller's grinning face and folksy humour before an estimated 20 million viewers a week.

The very tall Schuller shook my hand and, after asking our nationality, encouraged us on our way down to the

Jordan, where I was baptised by my new friend, Salvation Army officer Rodney Stevens. It was so special to me, knowing and understanding full well, what I was doing.

Ruben the Hebrew

'Ladies and gentlemen, over on ze slopps, ve have ze aypells growing.'

'Hey, Ruben! Those are apples growing on the slopes, not aypells on ze slopps!'

Ruben was our Jewish tour guide, who gave us a commentary on both the historic sites and the advancement of modern Israel, with its many orchards and areas of reforestation since modern Israel gained its independence in 1948.

Ruben was small in stature but large in personality, with a thick Hebrew accent and dry sense of humour. I found him a likeable character.

When we arrived at the Dead Sea, Ruben, after his commentary informing us that this was the lowest point on Planet Earth, bragged how, in his time as a lifeguard at the Dead Sea, he never had any swimmers drown on his watch.

We were advised to take off any rings or jewellery before floating on the heavily salted water. It was 1984 and, being interested in all things Jewish; I was aware of their current war in Lebanon where the IDF had occupied Beirut to rout out the PLO, led by Yasser Arafat.

I asked Ruben if he had been in the military during Israel's conflicts of the Six-Day War and Yom Kippur War. His simple answer was, 'Yes, all Israelis who were healthy and of age, involved in defending our God-given homeland, fighting for the survival of our fledgling nation.'

Conscription exists in Israel for all citizens over the age of 18 who are Jewish, Druze or Circassian; but not Arab citizens of Israel. The normal length of compulsory service

Chapter 7 DOUBTS AT THE RIVER JORDAN

is two years and eight months for men (with some roles requiring an additional four months of service) and two years for women.

Ruben had been a part of the 1967 IDF that had liberated the old city of Jerusalem, particularly the western wall or the wailing wall, the remnant of the Jewish Temple and the holiest place in Judaism, liberated for the first time in 1900 years.

We visited Yad Vashem, Israel's official memorial to the victims of the Holocaust and the Shrine of the Book, the home of several exceptional finds such as the Dead Sea Scrolls and other rare ancient manuscripts. Then we travelled back down to our Kibbutz near the Sea of Galilee.

It was to be our last night with Ruben. I felt privileged to be sitting at the same table with him, as our group dined in a restaurant overlooking the sea. The menus were written in Hebrew, English and French.

I had a go at pronouncing some Hebrew words and asked Ruben, 'How did I go?' He smiled. 'Aypells!'

I'll never forget the day of my water baptism, signifying the laying down of my old self, my old ways. Into a new self, and a new way, God's way, I felt loved, needed, and accepted, by the Creator of the Universe that I wholeheartedly followed Christ Jesus my Saviour into the waters of baptism, after all, He had saved me, healed me, and set me free, giving me abundant and eternal life!

Chapter 8

NEVER ALONE

My friend Bill was so excited and fired up in his Christian faith. On the same night that we found out about the Tour to Israel, I heard for the first time about this mystery called the Holy Spirit. There was talk about speaking in tongues and baptism in the Holy Spirit but not an explanation of what 'it' was or as they said "He" was. Bill tried to describe to me this fantastic feeling that he'd experienced when he had initially 'spoken' in other tongues. I didn't understand it, but I did want that feeling.

Again, I'd found myself up the front of the meeting; some people laid their hands on me and prayed for me to *receive* the baptism of the Holy Spirit. They explained that the evidence would be that I, too, would begin speaking in other tongues. They suggested I keep repeating, 'Hallelujah! Hallelujah!'

There was no wonderful feeling and no speaking in other tongues for me, but as we drove home, Bill encouraged me not to give up. I felt so disappointed, I didn't understand what baptism in the Holy Spirit meant, but something had stirred inside of me. A hunger within me to get to know God and all that He was.

A hunger to seek Him for who He is, not just for the temporal emotional feeling that I may or may not get. I used to hunger after only that which satisfied me, *and* I still fought with the *thirst* for the next feel-good experience fuelled by alcohol. This lifestyle change was so hard. It is one thing to 'decide' to lay your old ways, but certainly another to action that!

Some time passed between by water baptism in Israel and my experience of baptism in the Holy Spirit. I often thought back to the night in the hall when they prayed over me for the baptism in the Holy Spirit, and nothing happened. But over time, I became mindful of the Holy Spirit.

Then one day…I was driving to work to start an afternoon shift at Lysaght's. Once again, my thoughts drifted to that of the Holy Spirit. I decided to express my joy to God speaking 'Hallelujah' (which means praise the Lord), over and over, but this time it wasn't by rote or because someone told me to. I was praising God, not just following a formula. I was alone with God and feeling no inhibitions, and I meant each word.

There were no church songs in the background; no preacher praying over me, just myself and God in the car. Suddenly, I burst into a language I didn't understand. Words cannot describe the wonderful presence that filled the car. It was like heaven had opened the door of my car and sat in the front seat. I continued to speak these words; they seemed to come from deep within my heart; unrecognisable words, flowing out of my mouth like a fountain.

My eyes flooded with tears of joy. It was *my* mouth, *my* tongue, *my* lips and *my* breath, but a God-given language only my Spirit could understand, *and* I realised that I was not alone.

From this day on, my thirst changed. I began to be thirsty, not for alcohol or a sensation, but God Himself!

***

The Hot Strip

I was changing from the inside out, learning new ways of doing things. I felt blessed and confident that God was

Chapter 8   NEVER ALONE

with me and leading my life. I moved back on to shift work, earning better money and loved my new job on the galvanising line as a crane driver and maintenance assistant.

I worked in well with the mainly Dutch fitters and their assistants on C crew, even learning a few Dutch words. I was interested in understanding something of their lives back in Holland.

The hierarchy demanded cutbacks, and therefore some fitters and trades assistants were moved to various parts of the Westernport Plant. Their policy was last on, first off. We were informed that it was coming, but I had thought that since God was leading my life through the Holy Spirit, there was no way he would let me lose the job I loved so much. *But,* 'Sorry to be losing you, Vic, but with the financial cutbacks, we have had to restructure the galvanising line mechanical department.'

I got the short straw and was told to report for duty to the dreaded **hot strip** mill roll shop. It was the noisiest, greasiest, hottest part of Lysaght's, where the machinists resurfaced the massive backup rolls and work rolls.. The 100-tonne overhead electric crane was three stories above the workshop floor and would groan, and creak as the massive 80-tonne backup rolls were moved off and on the huge lathes for resurfacing. It was a hard, unfriendly place, and it seemed to me those who worked there were hard and unfriendly too.

It was during a nightshift meal break I felt prompted by the Holy Spirit to witness to them about my Christianity. My immediate thoughts were how embarrassing it would be when they found out I wasn't the big tough bloke I was making out to be. But after I quietly prayed, I gained the courage to witness to them. It was awkward and uncomfortable, but I had a moment with each of them individually.

The next evening night shift, I had just relieved the previous crane operator. Seated high above the roll shop, I saw that a few of the ground crew riggers had put together a makeshift wooden cross. One of them dragged it across the workshop floor right in front of me. They thought it was a great joke in response to my witnessing to them about my new-found Christianity. I was embarrassed, angry, and felt helpless. My default before Christ, was to become violent and aggressive, both verbally and physically when my pride was challenged. In the end, I got out of the hot strip roll shop and even left on relatively friendly terms because I hadn't reacted in a negative way to the cheeky ground crew riggers. It served as one of the first of many lessons to start doing things God's way and not react the old Victor Krone way.

What was that Language?

There was a job vacancy back on the galvanising line paying more money. A line operator was needed, so I was transferred from mechanical to production. I was still on C crew, where Andrew Gibson was the foreman. I was so glad to be back on the nice, clean and comparatively quiet galvanising line.

I had just completed my part in the process and done my checks and engaged the next coil. It was an afternoon shift—about 9:00 pm. Not many workers were around, and there were 35 minutes before the next coil. I was feeling blessed and started speaking to and praising God in my new heavenly language. I had my eyes closed and had been going for about five minutes when I felt a pat on my arm; it was the foreman.

My first thoughts were to wish that the concrete floor would swallow me! I hadn't remembered that the foreman rode a quiet pushbike to get around the large galvanising line, so I had no warning for me to stop speaking before he came. I didn't know how long he'd had been there listening, but he asked, 'What was that language?'

Chapter 8 NEVER ALONE

I didn't yet know and understand a lot of the bible, but the words of Jesus I had read the previous day came to me in an instant. *"Everyone who acknowledges me publicly here on earth, I will also acknowledge before my Father in heaven. But everyone who denies me here on earth, I will also deny before my Father in heaven."* (Matthew 10:32–33). So, I gathered my courage and replied, 'It's a spiritual language, and it happened after I recently became a born-again Christian.' He didn't comment any further, but I noticed he had a curious look on his face as he rode off.

After sharing my faith on many occasions at Lysaght's, I connected with other fellow Christians. Some of my work friends would tell me where these Christians were because they had shared their faith with them too.

Andrew was a young electrical apprentice. He too had recently become a Christian, baptised in the Holy Spirit, and was very bold in witnessing, but not so wise in his style. He often confronted other workers about their 'sinful' lifestyles in a way that was very 'in their face.'

Andrew soon learnt that confronting people in such a way was not necessarily an effective way to evangelise. For example, in the lunchroom, the blokes would look at porn magazines and have nude pictures on the walls. Andrew would rip them down and throw them in the bin. Even on the walls of the toilet cubicles, there were rude drawings or filthy language. He wrote scripture next to their filth and got into toilet wall debates.

Andrew had led a comparatively sheltered life, being raised in a Catholic family. Gentle natured and well-mannered. His passion for sharing His faith was commendable, but he was a little naïve and certainly not streetwise. On the other hand, I knew a lot about these blokes and their lifestyles because I had been on both sides of the street. I wasn't their judge, but I knew the pain and loneliness of that lifestyle and that it would never satisfy.

It was an afternoon shift meal break I was sitting with the blokes that owned the girly magazines and the nude pictures on the lunchroom wall that Andrew had ripped down and thrown in the bin. One of these blokes said to the other, 'Let's get the f****ing mongrel.'

While the Holy Spirit was with Andrew and protecting him; he was also teaching him. I felt God used me to come alongside Andrew and stand up to the tough blokes, not in a belligerent way, but these blokes knew what I was like before I'd become a Christian and didn't want to mess with me. They were surprised when I said, 'Leave him alone. He's my friend!'

Steve was another of the Christians I'd come to know. He'd worked at Lysaght's for many years and knew other Christians who worked there too. 'Do you know Ray?' he asked.

A Man Named Ray

Ray was one of the first persons ever to try and witness to me back in the day. What a difficult time I gave him. I remember it being one frosty morning, with the sun peeking over the horizon, a promise of a fantastic summer's day. I had been allocated to work with Ray, a fitter I had never met before.

After carrying all the tools and equipment up five levels, we looked out at the magnificent view.

'Isn't that beautiful out there?' I said.

'Yes, and a beautiful person created it,' he replied.

His words grated against me, and I came back at him with my rebuttal, as I wanted to defend my atheism.

'You don't believe all those fairy tales in the bible, do you?'

Chapter 8 NEVER ALONE

'Yes,' Ray said politely. 'It's God's word. The truth.'

Funny, I remember thinking that this guy was a 'religious nut' and yet here I am thinking and believing the same way. I reacted to Ray, but the same way that the guys had reacted to Andrew (even though his faith-sharing method was not confronting or combative. I talked him down, laughed and scoffed at him, using as many swear words I possibly could. But Ray didn't get upset or react negatively. He got on with the job we were doing. I couldn't relate to Ray, even his lifestyle modelled a faith I didn't understand; He didn't even drink or smoke! Even though I didn't recognise it then, I realise now that Ray had shown me grace, not judgement, just grace.

'You have got to be joking! Not the fitter?'
'Yes, he has finished up at Lysaght's, and he is now a full-time pastor.'
'I don't think he likes me, not the way I treated him back then.'

Steve told me that Ray pastored at a local Pentecostal church that met in the Uniting Church building in Hastings and that amazing things were happening in people's lives.

'Do you want to attend a service with me and maybe see Ray?'

We arrived a bit after 10:00 am one morning, and the little church was full. I could see Ray up the front preaching. I honestly didn't think he would notice me, but after the service, he said, 'When I saw you, the thought crossed my mind of how anti-Christian you had been and wondered if you had come intending to make trouble here today.'

69

Whilst Ray hadn't been the person who led me to the Lord through his witness (because I wasn't ready to listen), I believe that the Holy Spirit had used him knowing that one day I would look back and remember the truth of what he'd tried to tell me and the manner in which he did. I found out later that Pastor Ray, along with many other Christians, had been praying for the whole western port area, including Lysaght's Hastings. They had been praying for me, and I didn't even know it. I, along with many others, were set free, saved, healed, and became disciples of Jesus Christ because of their prayers.

Big Wayne

Wayne was a no-nonsense, straight-talking six-foot-five Tasmanian. He had been an axeman in Tassie and had worked hard on the land doing farm work. The span of his calloused hands was huge and could make a big fist. You would NEVER argue with big Wayne!

When he moved to the mainland from Tasmania to work for Lysaght's Hastings, we met and became friends. Wayne and I would often drink together and share each other's sorrows as he too, had separated from his wife, but after I became a Christian and shared my new faith with him our friendship ended.

It took some time for me to pluck up enough courage to awkwardly tell him the reason why I wasn't drinking anymore - I had become a born-again Christian. He said to me in his deep serious voice, 'I don't want anything to do with that crap.' I didn't argue. We didn't see each other.

***

My life was certainly going in a different direction. I was now a regular church-goer (who would've thunk it!) attending

Chapter 8 NEVER ALONE

the local church called Dandenong Assembly of God led by Pastor Alun Davies. Lindy was supportive of my journey of faith, but not ready for regular church meetings (although she did occasionally attend with me. I found myself hating shift work, and I had a strong desire to know and understand the Bible more. So, with Lindy's blessing, of "God is with us," I enrolled in a local night-time bible school and resigned from Lysaght's via an exit interview. I often think about the irony of that because in all my working life, every job I just walked into with no job interview process. Now, as a Christian, I had an interview, albeit an exit interview!

After enrolling, I rang Bill to ask if he knew of any day work for me. He had finished at Lysaght's too and had gone back to his bricklaying. He said he would get me on as a brickie's labourer. I had never done it before but was willing to give it a go. I was in my mid-thirties, quite strong, but overweight and not very fit, having sat on my backside crane operating for the last four years.

The job nearly killed me! Keeping the mud up to six brickies, especially when it had to be mixed, barrowed and shovelled up two levels of scaffolding, wow!

Bill could see I was battling, and said he had a mate in a sand soil and mini mix concrete yard in Dandenong, known as 'Dandy Mini Mix'. A Christian family owned it, and Bill's mate, Kevin, was the son-in-law of the owner and the manager of the yard. It was not good money, but I felt at home truck driving.

It was day work, and the blokes I worked with were Christians, albeit a bit rough around the edges. But I was 'God's work in progress!' Often I would lose my temper and let certain language slip.

Bill started driving with us too. Quite often, it was the two of us running the yard as Kevin, who was a troubled Vietnam veteran, was a binge drinker and would get on the alcohol and not turn up for a few days.

I had been travelling to Dandenong for bible school and work for about 12 months. Lysaght's and shift work had become a distant memory until our neighbour, Gwen, who lived opposite us and was working at Lysaght's, asked if I had heard about big Wayne. 'He has been off work and is not very well.'

I felt a deep conviction that I should go and visit Wayne and share with him *again* about God's love. I sensed the Holy Spirit leading me on this mission. I took Gideon's student bible with the New Testament, Psalms and Proverbs, and with the all-important sinner's prayer on the back page.

I started praying in tongues, and by the time I had travelled the 25 minutes to Wayne's house at Bittern, I felt energised and confident that God was with me. My fears of being rejected by man, were well and truly overcome because of my strong faith in God, through the Holy Spirit's encouragement.

I hadn't spoken to Wayne since leaving Lysaght's a couple of years before. Our friendship had come to a grinding halt after I had shared my new faith with him. I hadn't been to his newly built house, nor had I met his partner, nor had I met her big dogs!

Wayne's house was built at the rear of an acre block. The only entrance was through a traditional large swinging farm gate. I was about halfway to the front door when I saw two large dogs coming at me. They didn't bark or growl, but like attack dogs, were on to me in a heartbeat. I knew I was in big trouble, but, miraculously, they stopped with their snouts on my upper legs but no teeth. I froze for a few seconds and, then caught my breath, feeling extremely relieved to be still alive and unharmed, I continued to the front door.

After knocking, Wayne's surprised partner came to the door and asked in an alarmed tone, 'How did you get past the dogs?'

Chapter 8   NEVER ALONE

When Wayne heard my voice, I was invited in for a cuppa and introduced to his partner. It was sad to see my friend, who had been strong and healthy, eaten away with cancer, and in a lot of pain, but he offered a friendly handshake and seemed glad to see me.

During this timely visit, Wayne showed an openness as he received the Gideon's New Testament with the all-important sinner's prayer.

Big Wayne was terminally ill and passed from this life one week later. But I thank God for His grace and mercy that the power of the Holy Spirit broke through many barriers getting to the heart of this rugged Tasmanian axeman. Big Wayne, who had said, 'I don't want anything to do with that crap' had, I believe, after praying the sinner's prayer, received Jesus as Saviour and Lord!

Baptism in the Holy Spirit is not a 'religious' experience. My old self would've laughed at what I was embracing now. But no one can ever tell me different – because, from that day onwards, I found that I was never alone.

There is much to the Holy Spirit, and this isn't the book to describe all that He is, but I will say this; there have been numerous times (more than the stories shared in this chapter), since receiving the baptism in the Holy Spirit that I have been reminded of Jesus's love for me, His acceptance of me and that I've never had to face anything alone.

In some situations, He has reminded me of a Bible verse that has encouraged me, other ways, He provided comfort in difficult situations and other times, he gave me the right words to share this faith that had set me free, with others. He gave me the courage to rise above rejection of man and share my faith again. And still, other times to share the right words to comfort or encourage someone else.

The Bible tells us that Jesus said, "If anyone thirsts, let him come to Me and drink. He who believes in Me, as the Scripture has said, out of his heart will flow rivers of living water." Jesus was talking about the Holy Spirit. (John 7:37–39 NJKV.) I had lost my thirst, not only for alcohol, but for the all the temporary fixes to which I used to default.

Jesus also said of the Holy Spirit, "But the Helper will teach you everything, and will cause you to remember all that I told you. This Helper is the Holy Spirit whom the Father will send in my Name". (John 14:26 NCV).
The Holy Spirit has been a constant helper in my life, and now I live life with absolute confidence that I'm Never Alone!

Dad H.M.A.S Australia WW2

Mum in her late teens in Melbourne during WW2

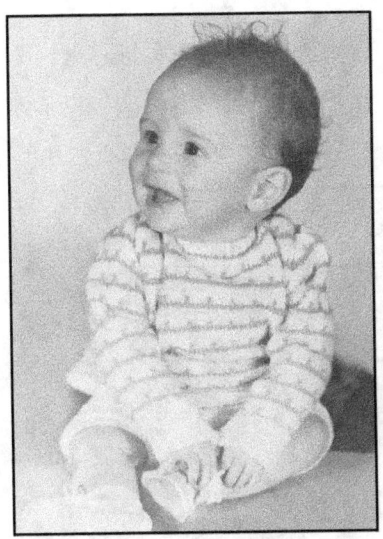
Vic at nine months

Vic and sister Lyn 2 and 3 years

I AM' ARRESTED

Grandfather Charlie, Nanny Millie, little Victor, Mum & Uncle Charlie

Floating bridge - Southampton

118 Stitches In Face

Doctors and nurses at Prince Henry's Hospital are proud of the wonderful recovery of a small boy who was knocked down by a truck a week ago yesterday.

And particularly are they proud of the wonderful work the surgeon has done on the child's face.

The boy, brown-eyed Victor Krone, aged 16 months, was brought to the hospital with his face shockingly lacerated.

The surgeon worked 2¾ hours stitching it together and in all put 118 stitches in the little face.

Today, with even the marks of the stitches disappearing, Victor was full of grins as he clasped a small rag doll.

He has become such a pet that he now objects strongly when other patients get attention.

He will have to remain in hospital some weeks because he also has a fractured leg, but he is well on the way to recovery, and already has his good looks back.

Boy, 3, gets £1000 for broken leg

A THREE-YEAR-OLD boy, knock-kneed since his leg was broken when he was hit by a truck in April last year, was awarded £1000 damages in the Supreme Court yesterday.

The boy, Victor Charles Krone, of Bay-st., Port Melbourne, sued the owners of the truck, Canada Cycle & Motor. Co. (Vic.) Pty. Ltd., and the driver, through his father.

The action was settled out of court. Mr. Justice Dean, entering judgment, directed that the bulk of the £1000 be invested in trust for the boy.

News paper clippings of the accident

Mary Key the Mayor of Southampton meeting the Queen

Vics baptism at the river Jordan

Vic and kids passport photo 1975

Vic and adult kids from left to right Jason, Karen, Brendan, Vic, Leanne, Shane.

Vic and Lindy on their wedding day with Mum and Lindys Dad Reg

Vic and Lindy at Frankston Community Church

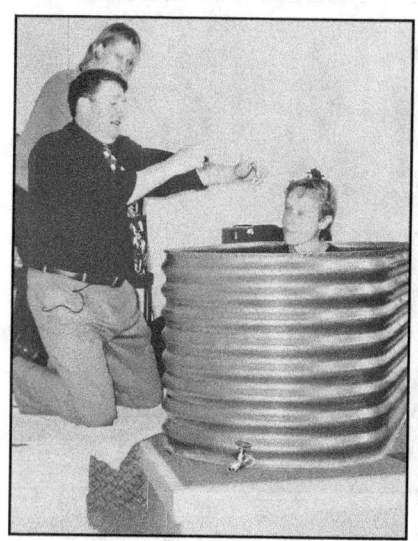
Baptism's at Teen Challenge

A message of hope at Teen Challenge

Chapter 9

LEARNING, GROWING & SERVING

Frankston TAFE

Meryl was the business manager at Frankston TAFE. The newly formed tertiary college had transitioned from secondary education, originally opening as Frankston High School in 1926. Then on the fourth of February 1958, with 275 students, it changed to become Frankston Technical School. The Frankston Technical College, by constitution, officially became the Frankston College of TAFE on 29th September 1981.

Meryl also ran a small catering business for weddings and social functions, and needed some workers to wait on tables and clean up. Lindy and I worked for Meryl on quite a few occasions, it was challenging work, but a bit of extra money that we needed. We were run off our feet, but we enjoyed it and would often have a good laugh afterward at some of the embarrassing moments, like the thumb in the soup or the soup in the lap or on one occasion, as Lindy ashamedly confesses, down the back of a senior citizen's coat!

After nearly 12 months of travelling to Dandenong for work and attending night bible school, Meryl asked Lindy, who had been working at Frankston TAFE as a part-time cleaner for six months, if I would be interested in a cleaning job too. It was a full-time position and could start the following week. Little did I know just about how much my life was going to change, and what incredible direction it would take me.

Frankston Community Church

I loved my new job at Frankston College of TAFE. I was willing to go the extra mile and would take up the challenges given to me and do the 'too hard basket' things, many times working after hours. I started as a cleaner and worked my way up to 'supervisor'. I eventually acted as the assistant facilities manager, which required me, at times, to sit in meetings on the college council.

The college was still developing, with growing student numbers requiring more teaching and support staff. Consequently, we had to build new facilities and renovate existing ones to accommodate them; creating a logistical challenge with the furniture, equipment, security, and safety, for not only the main campus, but the four annexed facilities at Rosebud, Carrum Downs, Kookaburra Street in Frankston, and Bonbeach.

Amazingly, I found myself in a position of trust and responsibility. God had opened a window of opportunity for me to share my faith on many levels. I was asked by the editor of the Frankston TAFE in-house newspaper (*Quality News*) to write a short story on my life's journey before starting at TAFE.

After the article was published, which included my born-again Christian conversion, I was approached by other Christians in the college to join and eventually run a Christian fellowship group. It was open to, mainly teaching and support staff, and some interested students, one of whom was Anthony, a mechanical engineering student who, with our group's prayer and support, introduced 'Students for Christ' to the campus.

Chapter 9 LEARNING, GROWING & SERVING

I was still travelling from Frankston to Dandenong Assemblies of God for evening services and loved the great preaching of Ps Alun Davies, but I'd never gotten involved in the life of the local church, to be mentored, to serve or to learn discipleship, but this was going to change, and soon.

God's Favour

At the same time, a church called Springvale Assembly of God was looking to start a church in Frankston under the leadership of Pastor Uwe (Ian) Kruithoff. They had set out to start a church in Frankston and had their first meetings at Chisholm (now known as Monash University), in Frankston, but the doors closed on the hire of that venue after 12 months. But God was about to open another one.

I was acting as the assistant facilities manager at Frankston TAFE and first met Pastor Ian when he enquired about hiring the TAFE auditorium for their church meetings. He mentioned he had been praying to God for a larger, more central venue for the church and strongly believed it was the Frankston TAFE auditorium, as it was central, close to public transport, and had plenty of parking. But there was already a social group with a long-term booking using it every second Sunday, so it looked like it was not going to work. But Pastor Ian and his team didn't give up, and they *prayed* that this venue would be open to them.

Their prayers were answered; the social group with the long-term booking suddenly finished up, leaving the TAFE auditorium clear for Sunday morning and evening services. Services that Lindy and I would begin to attend. Services that would be God's provision for Lindy and me to learn and grow in our Christian faith and prepare us for future ministry. It made sense for me to attend this church since I lived in Frankston and worked at TAFE. Later, Lindy joined regularly. We found new life in this community church. We found a place to serve, grow, be discipled and loved in. We found a place of belonging!

***

In Jesus' Name

'Hey Vic, we, can't hold off any longer. The baptismal candidates and Pastor Ian are ready now!' The TAFE auditorium had an elevated stage with a large blue curtain across the front that was to be kept closed until the baptisms started.

We had borrowed a portable galvanised tub and filled it to well over the halfway mark with hot water from TAFE's huge boilers. I had naively thought I would just put in some cold water in the last few minutes before the baptisms started. Wrong! The critical mass of hot water didn't seem to cool down very much. The packed church with lots of visitors had no idea that behind the curtain, the bucket brigade frantically tried to displace the hot with cold to get it ready for the baptisms.

The first person was a young woman who was a trophy of God's grace. She had recently been saved and delivered from years of drug and alcohol abuse. As she sat in the tub and felt the heat of the water, she said, 'Jesus, it's hot!' Pastor Ian quickly replied, 'That's it, praise Jesus!' Most people burst into laughter. I don't know if she was praising the Lord or notifying him of the water temperature.

***

I had been in our bedroom and thought I could hear from the television in the lounge about this great New Zealand revival. I ran to hear the rest of this exciting news, only to realise they were advertising New Zealand cheeses!

Chapter 9 LEARNING, GROWING & SERVING

I had come to love and honour the name of Jesus and felt hurt when I heard his name blasphemed. In fact, at one stage, I thought it was my duty to protect his name.

Will was one of our maintenance electricians at TAFE, a likeable bloke who got on well with the other workers, but he let me know on many occasions that he wasn't going to hold back on his language just because I was a Christian. One time just before he walked outside, he let out a tirade, using Jesus as a swear word. I became angry and punched the wall!

Will didn't see, but God did and instantly convicted me of being a hypocrite as he reminded me of my behaviour one time when I was drunk in the public bar of the Westernport Hotel in Hastings. The Salvation Army officers came into the bar and were handing out their Christian pamphlet, *War Cry*. In my drunken stupor, I asked, 'What's that all about?'

They replied with what was probably a civil answer; I can't recall. But when the name Jesus was mentioned, the two Salvation Army officers began to back away when this angry, six-foot-two, 18-stone drunk stood over them. Speaking in a serious tone, I said, 'I am Jesus!'

Stolen Goods

The Holy Spirit was gently leading my life. In the Aussie subculture, my understanding was it's okay to pilfer a few bits and pieces from the workplace, just don't get caught! I felt convicted that some of the stolen goods I had pilfered during my working life were still in my possession. I got rid of it and turned my hands to helping and giving. Paul taught the Church at Ephesus, *if you are a thief, quit stealing. Instead, use your hands for good hard work, and then give generously to others in need.* (Ephesians 4:28). This is how I met Dot.

Dot

Dot was an English lady who had migrated to Australia with her husband, Ron. She became a Christian and started attending our church at TAFE. She had heard some of my testimony and asked if I would pray for and then meet her husband, to encourage him with the hope that he might become a Christian too.

Ron was a cheeky little cockney. I shared some of my journey with him, including my new conviction on pilfering from the workplace. Afterwards, he leant over and quietly said in his cockney accent, "'ere, Guv, cooden do tha! Down at me work, I likes ta nick a few nuts and bolts.'

Big Jock

Frankston North, in particularly "The Pines," was a lower socioeconomic area, with substantial government housing, a higher-than-average crime rate, and population of approximately 5500. I believed, in God's economy, Lindy and I were strategically positioned in a field mission for a season. And, that was where big Jock lived in a caravan, at the rear of his mum's house.

We had been visiting a lady named Maria. She had been wonderfully saved and set free through the City Life Ministry, which was the welfare arm of our church. It provided emergency food hampers, clothing, and hope for those with life-controlling problems. She was keen to see others set free too, so as we were leaving, she said, 'See that big man with the shaved head sitting on next door's lawn', I have started praying for him, his name is Big Jock!'

Jock, 37 years old, was a fearsome sight with his shaved head and heavily tattooed body that weighed 222 kg (35 stone). It was a sweltering day as Jock sat topless, wearing his huge yellow tracksuit pants, drinking beer straight from

Chapter 9   LEARNING, GROWING & SERVING

a long neck. As I drove away from Maria's house, my thoughts were, *'God will have to do the miraculous for that bloke to change'*. Oh, me of little faith!

'Hey Vic, do you remember the next-door neighbour I was praying for?'

'Big Jock?'

'Yes, he wants to come to church this Sunday.'

Our Mazda 626 sedan's manual gear lever was almost impossible to change when Jock sat beside me as a front-seat passenger, as there was a lot of overhang! He couldn't fit through the rear door to sit on the back seat.

Jock had been left disabled after a bad car accident when he was 18. He could no longer play football or work as a panel beater, so he would eat and drink all day. Consequently, the following 20 years of over-eating and drinking had taken an even greater toll on his morbidly obese body. But this was not a problem for God. Jock came to church and felt God's love and grace, and he invited Jesus into His heart, food and beer had lorded his life long enough. It was an unforgettable Sunday, reminding me again of what God did for me and his love to do the same for others! We continued to taxi him to meetings, and he became a good friend, spending a lot of time at our home.

One sweltering summer, Lindy and I would most days arrive home at lunchtime and have a dip in our Clark's pool to cool off before going back to work. It was half in the ground with a timber deck around one end. Jock would get a taxi to our place and be in the pool from 10.00 am until we arrived home at lunchtime. He put a chair into the pool so he could step up and roll himself on to the deck.

One day we drove into our driveway at 4.00 pm after work and could hear a noise coming from the rear of our property. 'Help! Help! I'm out here!' We went out to find

Jock stuck in the pool, unable to get out. He was like a giant prune! After spending six hours in the pool, he was thirsty, hungry, and cold. He quickly downed a couple of bottles of diet coke, a pot of soup, a loaf of bread, and a cup of coffee. Then he finally warmed up.

Jock's doctor warned him, if he kept eating the way he did, he would only survive six months. After three months, he got down to 127 kg from 222kg and was able to have his first bath in 10 years. It wasn't because he preferred to shower; it was because he couldn't find a bath big enough. Jock shared how the first month was agony, especially in the first ten days, he lost a staggering 38 kg (six stone) by drinking water and eating salad. God is interested in our daily battle; even in this Jock was not alone.

Against all the odds, he lived for another two years before he passed away from terminal cancer. His last conversation with me occurred a couple of days before he passed, reminding me that faith is uncomplicated. Jock believed God loved Him and was not troubled with his death sentence. What a privilege it was for me to pray for Him, and I sensed that the Holy Spirit had given Jock a peace in his heart – he was going home *to His eternal home.*

At Jock's funeral, I confidently shared with his family and friends that he was in heaven with Jesus, because he had received by faith what God had done through His Son, Jesus Christ, in paying the price for the sins of the entire world, and that it was available for them too. About 12 months later, Jock's family contacted me and asked me to visit his mum, Margaret, who was also terminally ill with cancer. Margaret had been a victim of abuse and had been deserted and left to raise her three sons as a single parent. That very night she gave her heart to the Lord. She received God's love and forgiveness and the grace to forgive, and in turn, received peace, freedom, ultimate healing and the promise of eternal life.

Chapter 9 LEARNING, GROWING & SERVING

Robinsons Road

Frankston Community Church was pioneered in 1985 by a young Ps Uwe (Ian) Kruithoff, who initially had few human resources and even less in financial resources at his disposal. Amazingly, under his leadership, within five years, we had purchased 6.5 acres of land, built a church building, and had grown to over 350 attendees, many of whom had sacrificially given their time and money. Soon it would be time to build and leave the hired TAFE facility.

I was still working at TAFE during the process of building our new facility at Robinsons Road. We were permitted to borrow a lot of tools, equipment, and furniture during the 12 months it took to complete our church building. At one stage, there was so much furniture and equipment moving between the Frankston TAFE main campus and our building site that it was often referred to, sometimes mockingly by my co-workers, as 'Robinsons Road TAFE'.

A Mammoth Job

We were blessed to have a handful of tradies in our midst, but most of us were just there to help in whatever way we could. When nearing the completion of the project, our drainer/plumber needed a hand to have a stormwater drain connected to our property. A large machine was required to bore under the main road adjacent to our property. Then, under his instruction, we were to push the 12-inch stormwater pipe about ten metres through the freshly bored hole, while standing in a pit that was a metre deep. It seemed like it would be a straightforward process.

My understanding was that the shortest distance between two points is a straight line, but we soon realised that the underground bore, while it went from point A to point B, wasn't a straight line. It had a slight bend. That was challenging enough, but just as we started to insert the pipe into place, the heavens opened, and we were soaked and covered in mud. We yelled out to the plumber over the other side of the road,

> 'It's not going in!'
> 'Pull it out and push it in,' he yelled back.

So, both myself and the associate Pastor at the time, Jurgen were covered in mud, freezing cold, with rain dripping off our noses, we pulled the pipe out and tried to push it back in. I felt we needed something to lighten the heavy moment, so, with my weird sense of humour, I turned and said to Jurgen, 'I imagine this would be what it's like to artificially inseminate a dinosaur!'

It's not that funny now; I guess you had to be there, in a hole holding a giant heavy pipe; but we laughed until we cried, although you wouldn't have noticed since we were soaking wet and covered in mud. Job well done!

Philippines

As well as building our new church facilities, Ps Ian knew the importance of team building and training disciples. Our leadership group was encouraged to go on a short-term mission and an opportunity came up in the Philippines through world missions.

A couple named Brian and May, both Chinese Singaporeans had planted a church and started a bible college in Laoag City in the province of Ilocos Norte, Philippines. Brian, like myself, had been set free from a long-term addictive lifestyle of heroin addiction, he truly understood the grace of God through Christ Jesus and wanted others to know the same. Both were passionate about taking the good news they had received to the poor people of Ilocos Norte.

Chapter 9   LEARNING, GROWING & SERVING

At our briefings, we were advised to be mindful of Muslim rebels who may come into one of the churches out in the barrios where some of us would be ministering. There had been recent kidnappings, and missionaries had been murdered when ransom demands weren't met. That information didn't make us feel all warm and fuzzy. 'You will have a chance to preach,' do communion, pray for the sick, do hospital visits, and share your personal story. Be praying, because the battle is not in only what we see, it's also a spiritual battlefield we're going into.'

After arriving at Manila's Ninoy Aquino International Airport, we were taken on a hair-raising drive through chaotic traffic into a very hot Manila, with the options for transport being a tricycle, Jeepney or a battered excuse for a taxi. I had the latter. The trip made me think back to the crazy French doctor who had taken me into Paris, weaving in and out of traffic at a frantic pace and crash parking.

The next day we met up with an Aussie missionary named Chris. He and his wife were based in Manila and were helping the poorest of the poor, living on the infamous 'Smokey Mountain'; a garbage dump in Tondo Metro Manila where over 25,000 people picked up garbage for a living. Sadly, but not surprisingly, it's one of the most impoverished areas of the world.

Chris had not only learnt Tagalog, the common language of the Philippines but had learnt their version of road traffic rules. We were grateful that he drove us back through city traffic to the airport to catch a domestic flight down to Ilocos Norte. A couple of the others and I sat on the floor of his utility truck (obviously no seatbelts or airbags). He too drove like a madman, bashing and crashing and bluffing his way through the congested traffic. His disclaimer was, 'It's how you drive over here. If you don't drive with some force, you'll never get around.'

Hospital Visit

Most of our group were keen to get out and have a go. We'd heard of many miracles of healing, calling, and provision from others who had stepped out in missions. Where better than a hospital in a poor third world country to test our faith?

Laoag City Hospital was an eye-opener for me. The old buildings were rundown and in disrepair. The interior wardroom windowsills had layers of dust on them, breeding grounds for germs. There was no air conditioning, although some rooms had a fan. The hospital bed mattress was a block of foam rubber with stains of dried blood and other body fluids, no sheets or pillow slips. In stark contrast, the medical staff were all well-groomed, with spotlessly pristine uniforms.

We prayed for the sick and introduced the love of Jesus to many through the indigenous bible college students who were translating for us. We didn't see any *instant* healings, but it was reported to us later on, that some were healed!

The Outreach

Loaog City, with a population of around 100,000, had its fair share of people living on the streets, many affected by drug and alcohol abuse. Young Filipinos would leave their poor farming families out in the barrios of Ilocos Norte for the elusive excitement of city life and the hope of getting work and making their fortune. Most fell into the hands of criminals who would prey on their vulnerability and would entice them into prostitution, drug trafficking, and slavery.

It was Saturday evening in downtown Laoag City. The typically warm and humid air, was full of a combination of exhaust fumes and the smoky aroma of cooking food by the many street vendors. There was the sound of bustling crowds, the noisy overloaded tricycles and jeepneys, and the occasional man-powered rickshaw, combined with the clopping of pony hooves as they carried either goods or passengers in their primitive carts.

We prepared ourselves by praying and praising God before and during the outreach. Prayer and praise to God kept our perspective, reminding us that God is great even amidst poverty and in some places that just seemed evil. It was a great night with many hearing about Jesus and his love and grace for the first time. There were people healed from sickness and disease, and some even set free from spiritual oppression.

Crook as a Dog

Later that night, I began to feel incredibly unwell. I couldn't eat or drink anything, which was most unusual for me. It felt like two hands tightening around my neck. Breathing was difficult.

Ps Ian was a paramedic and his wife, Lorrie, a trained nurse. They reported that my pulse was rapid and shallow. I had never experienced anything like this. I didn't think it was my heart, although it was a possibility, being 41 and overweight and with symptoms that seemed heart-related.

I remembered seeing the conditions at the Laoag City hospital and my thoughts were that death was preferable, 'No, thanks. I'll go up to my bed and believe for healing.'

For the next 36 hours, I had the same painful choking feeling combined with heart palpitations, as I lay on my allocated bunk bed in the 35°C heat. The overnight temperature offered little relief as it would only drop down to about 29°C with no change in the 85% humidity. The only cooling was an old electric fan and a wet towel.

I realised that since being in the Philippines, I had eaten everything put in front of me without asking too many questions (not so wise). I had drawn the line at two local culinary items—balut, an 18-day-old fertilised duck egg, and dog! One time, after eating some delicious savoury meat served on their excuse for bread, they promised it wasn't dog meat. 'Hey Vic, you just ate a cultured earthworm.'

During the 36-hour ordeal in the oppressive heat, the guys on our team kept checking on me. They, along with the bible college students, prayed for me, and that night, after being anointed with oil and prayed over by our youth pastor Luke, I was healed!

20/20 Vision

I'm a slow learner, but during the pain of my 36-hour ordeal, while the Lord healed me, I knew I needed to start looking after my health. I had to stop overeating at every meal, change my eating habits, and get down to a healthier weight.

The accumulative effect of my 18-year alcoholic lifestyle had taken its toll on my health. As a new Christian, I now realised while I wasn't drinking alcohol and doing the many other destructive things associated with that lifestyle, I was overeating, including a lot of junk food. With the wisdom of hindsight, I have realised this was one of many lessons learnt the hard way. Pain is a good catalyst to get our attention.

Evil in our Neighbourhood

Back at home, there seemed to be a palpable fear in the atmosphere of the city of Frankston. I remember lying in bed, sensing the evil. The mutilated body of the latest victim a 17-year-old student named Natalie Russell was found lying under a couple of branches 300 metres from our home in Frankston North. She was the third within eight weeks.

The leaders of several churches around Frankston, including ours, had prioritised to unite in prayer and fasting for our city to be restored to a relatively safe place and that

Chapter 9 LEARNING, GROWING & SERVING

the police would have the wisdom and insight to apprehend this vicious, cruel murderer. My previous atheist belief would not have recognised this, but evil is very real. It fights against all that God had planned for His loved world. We felt as we prayed and fasted that there was a present satanic evil causing fear in our city. But we're never alone, and Jesus gave us a way to fight the unseen battle – the spiritual battle – battling for every soul. The Frankston Pastors continued to fight in prayer for their city.

In response to public alarm, police launched Operation Reassurance to increase their presence in the area and had planned to have 200 detective's door knock on the morning of 31st July. However, they had their breakthrough on Friday the 30th after a vigilant postman reported a suspicious man sitting in his vehicle on Skye Road, metres from where schoolgirl Natalie Russell was brutally murdered. The killer was captured; our prayer answered.

Being a Christian didn't remove fear or challenge from my life. It didn't remove the fact that evil fights for my soul. Why is the hope of eternal life so important to people like Jock and his Mum and all of us? Why do I have this drive to tell others about what the grace and love of Jesus? Why did I want to help build a church? Why did I want to share Jesus in the Philippines?

The simple answer, because having personally experienced God's love through Christ Jesus, I can love and serve others now because I see them through a different lens. I'm learning not to judge, use, and abuse, or figure out what I can get from others. I'm energised and fulfilled and feel amazingly privileged to love and serve others as I share the message of Jesus, which so richly lives, in my life.

Chapter 10

SOUTHAMPTON REVISITED

After ten years at Frankston TAFE, and serving on the leadership team at Frankston Community Church for around eight years, Lindy and I had made some lasting friendships. We were doing life with a great bunch of people. Most of us were relatively young and new to the Christian faith.

We had been on an exciting journey and at times, were stretched in our faith. We laughed and cried together and shared our homes for cell groups, prayer meetings, social nights around the BBQ or pool, and often taking in the lonely and broken-hearted, many with life-controlling addictions

Pastor Ian offered me a full-time position as an assistant pastor. It was all in God's timing, as the Frankston TAFE were offering a second round of voluntary departure packages. I wasn't considered in the first round, but after mentioning to my boss at TAFE about wanting to start as a full-time pastor, the door had opened.

Lindy and I had been married for ten years and hadn't had a honeymoon or a proper holiday. We had started our marriage carrying lots of personal baggage with many carryover financial debts. When I think of it now, from a human point of view, we were behind the eight-ball right from the start. Statistically, around half of first-time marriages end in divorce, and it compounds for second and third-time marriages. We had defied the odds to have lasted ten years. (As I'm writing, we are about to celebrate 34 years of marriage).

We defied the odds because we welcomed God into our daily lives, including our marriage and finances. We even had what we called a prayer life. Every struggle we had, we prayed to God for wisdom and help. Was it easy? No! Are we perfect now? NO!

Once Lindy and I attended a marriage enrichment seminar. The husband of the mature couple speaking announced that he and his wife had been married for 50 years and during that time hadn't had one disagreement! Much to the relief of us listening, the momentary silence of disbelief was broken by his words, 'We haven't had *one* disagreement, we've had thousands.'

One of the greatest challenges in marriage is often finances. We had agreed to trust God with our finances and actioned the step of faith by putting ten per cent of our income in the church offering bag each week. A great challenge many times over, sometimes even scary, especially while trying to pay off our debt, but we continued to exercise that faith, and it became something we don't even think about twice. God blessed us financially again and again.

It wasn't always logical how the bills got paid and that there were funds left over for fun or to give towards others, but God is beyond earthly budgets and His ways are certainly not ours, but so much greater than ours. God blessed us continually. We weren't rich in possession but rich with peace and satisfaction in what God has called us to do.

At one time we purchased a block of land in Port Sorrel on the north-east coast of Tasmania and managed to pay it out in 12 months. Soon after paying it out, we sold it for over three times what we had paid for it.

We had paid out our debts, renovated our home, built on a double brick garage, and with the payout from TAFE's

Chapter 10 SOUTHAMPTON REVISITED

voluntary departure package, we were able to buy another car and have our long-awaited honeymoon.

We based our 'honeymoon' in London, from where we enjoyed a coach tour around Western Europe, but there were three places we had prearranged that were, for me, ministry points. I had some unfinished business back in Southampton, which was the last, but, for me, the most important on our itinerary.

I had kept in touch with Jim Townsend, who I had befriended at Harvest Bible College. He and his wife, Anne, and their son and daughter had returned to Northern Ireland after completing their studies and had, with the support of their local Pentecostal church, set about trying to reach the youth on the streets of Belfast who were victims of the sectarian hatred and violence.

We were amazed to see the fortified police stations the army tanks in the CBD of Belfast and the heavily armed military guards at the many checkpoints.

Jim was raised in a Catholic family who lived in Belfast and knew the go and no go areas of Belfast and the Northern Island Counties.

He explained the two opposing areas divided by a peace wall were the Ardoyne which is a working-class and mainly Catholic and Irish nationalist district in north Belfast, Northern Ireland and the Shankill Road which is Protestant territory.

Jim met us at Belfast Airport and took us back to stay with them in their home in the suburbs of Belfast. I remember lying in bed that first night with a euphoric feeling. It was September 1994, and with the recently announced peace, I praised God and thanked Him for being with us, and that one-day forgiveness and reconciliation would bring about lasting peace in Northern Ireland.

Scottish Heritage

After leaving Belfast and the Townsend family, we travelled up into Southern Ireland, or the Free State, as the locals in Northern Ireland call it. We found the people warm and welcoming. We stayed in a 'bed and breakfast' accommodation, looked at many of the well-known tourist sites, and then flew back to London.

Both our maternal ancestral lines can be traced back to Scotland, in particular, to the highlands of Scotland. My ancestry leads to the Ross clan of Inverness and Lindy's to the Cameron clan of Fort William.

We just loved the Scottish Highlands with its beautiful lochs and met many friendly people in our B&B accommodation. We were enjoying our holiday and had many laughs making fun of each other's Scottish ancestors

> 'Ha! Your lot were uneducated Teuchters running around barefooted with William Wallace of *Braveheart* fame and his rabble. Whereas my lot were well educated and refined.'
>
> 'Whatever!

We were having a bit of fun with our friendly banter, but the Cameron Clan Museum at Achnacarry Castle near Fort William was very impressive.

After leaving the highlands of Scotland, we had arranged to visit our friend, Iris Wilson's dad, down in the hilly city of Dundee on our way to Manchester. Mr James Herschel greeted us with a friendly smile and asked in his distinctly Dundee accent, 'Arr ye the wee pastor and wife from Australia?'

After inviting us in, we knew we had the right person and address, when we noticed the familiar faces of the Wilsons in a lot of his photos on the wall. I don't think he knew

Chapter 10 SOUTHAMPTON REVISITED

what to expect, or how you're supposed to host a pastor. He was a lovely bloke and just wanted to please us because his daughter, Iris, was our friend.

I could sense he was trying to watch his Ps and Qs and I desperately wanted to tell him, 'It's okay, mate. I'm not the archbishop or the pope. I'm just a sinner who has received God's grace.'

After following this spritely old Scot up and down the hills of Dundee, we were both relieved to get to his local pub to catch our breath and sit down for lunch.

'Would ya like a pint?' he asked.

'No, thanks.' I was able to briefly share with Mr Herschel why I didn't drink alcohol. 'I used to drink one too many and got into lots of trouble, but out of the brokenness of that lifestyle, I found God, in whom I hadn't believed.'

'Oh, aye. Would ye like a cup o' tea?'

Ashton-under-Lyne

Bill and Lyn were among the group of church planters sent out from Springvale AOG to pioneer our church at Frankston. Lyn, a gifted pianist, had organised for Lindy and me to stay with her brother and sister-in-law, and then share my testimony with the church they had pioneered in Ashton-under-Lyne of Greater Manchester, England.

Pastor Stan Trees, a true Sydney boy, introduced me to their church before I gave my testimony and a gospel message. 'This is Vic. He's from Melbourne, where they have recently got electricity!'

They laughed when I replied, 'I went to Sydney once, and it wasn't open!'

After my message, a few people responded, and Pastor Stan and I prayed with them, some believing in Jesus for the first time, some deciding to revisit their faith and some even for healing. What a complete difference to what I was doing here last time!

We stayed with Stan and Ursula for a few days, during which time they showed us around Manchester. We did some DFO shopping (happy wife), and they drove us to the highest point overlooking Ashton-under Lyne.

Heading Home

After seven weeks of travel and living out of our suitcases, we'd seen more than our fair share of old castles and historic sites around Europe, Ireland and Britain and were ready to go home.

The last leg of our journey was Southampton where I wanted to see my ex-family members and let them *see* how God had changed my life, and to apologise for my disgusting behaviour towards them, and my own family while living in Southampton in the mid-1970s. I also had the hope of sharing my testimony with them, although my changed life was an undeniable witness to the power of God.

Some would ask, 'Would a normal person take his wife to visit his *ex*-mother-in-law while on his honeymoon/holiday?' My answer to that is if you've read this far, you would understand that for 18 years, I was not normal. I was foolish and, at times, insane. I wonder whether, by any standards, I'm normal now.

We had driven into Southampton from just outside of Bath, the historic Roman city and, with Lindy navigating, soon entered the familiar territory for me, of the Weston Estate and Mary's home, where I had stayed with my family for a short time in 1975.

Chapter 10 SOUTHAMPTON REVISITED

'Vic, we are only doing a quick visit, right?' Lindy asked.

'Yes, all good.'

Mary greeted us in her Midlands accent. 'Hello, it's good to see you both. Come in, and I'll make you a cuppa. Lindy, I've heard you like tea.'

Mary, being an influential character, combined with her skill in public speaking as two-time Mayor of Southampton, insisted we stay with her for a few days. 'You can have my room upstairs.'

The warm, accepting and generous hospitality shown by Mary, my ex-mother-in-law, and the gracious attitude shown by Lindy, my new wife, had the fingerprints of God's grace all over it.

The matriarch of the Key family had opened her door and welcomed us in, but God had opened the door for us to reconnect, share our faith and pray for the whole family.

Steps eight and nine of AA's 12 steps with their scriptural support say:

> *Evaluate all my relationships. Offer forgiveness to those who have hurt me and make amends for harm I've done to others when possible, except when to do so would harm them or others.*

> *"Happy are the merciful." (Matthew 5:7)*

> *"Happy are the peacemakers." (Matthew 5:9)*

Chapter 11

CHANGE & PROPHECY

It was hard to believe we'd racked up ten years at Frankston Community Church with Pastor Ian and the team. They had been years of learning and being stretched in our faith. We started to understand a lot about ourselves and what God can do with a willing heart that steps out in faith. We loved doing life with these guys who had sacrificially given to build *the* church (the building and the people in it).

Ps Jurgen and Connie, who had been our associate pastors at Frankston Community Church, had relocated and were now lead pastors at a smaller but growing church in Mooroolbark. They had been there for a while, when one day, they invited us to come and join them and assist them in transitioning into their recently purchased church facility. With a great measure of sadness in leaving the church that we 'had grown up in,' there was also a great sense of excitement, and we accepted their offer. We sold our home and purchased another home in Mooroolbark close to their church.

We lived in Mooroolbark for two years serving at the newly named Mooroolbark Neighbourhood Church with great adventure. And when the time had come, and the transition to the new facility completed, it was time to move again.

Hastings Short and Sweet

I had heard there was a need for a *lead* pastor at a church in Hastings. For the first time, I would be pastoring a church on my own. I cannot say 100% that God had smacked me over the head and said *'thou shalt go forth to Hastings'*, and I certainly wasn't going for the money, (cos there wasn't any), but we both agreed that it would be good to step out into the unknown and do our best with what God might have in store for us.

So with no idea of how long or short, this particular season would be, we both agreed to step out and have a go. There was a bonus incentive, our son and daughter-in-law, Jason and Charmaine, were youth leaders at the church, and this move meant being closer to them and the rest of our family. Pastor Len *Crone* was the lead pastor at the time, and I would be replacing him.

Not long after we'd moved to a new house and settled in the church, I re-connected with Ben, one of the Dutch fitters I'd known back in Lysaght's day. I was privileged to share my Christian faith and pray with Ben and his wife after him being diagnosed with terminal cancer. Just another reminder that 'God causes everything to work together for the good of those who love God and are 'called' according to his purpose for them'. (Romans 8:28). If we hadn't moved back, I wouldn't have had this opportunity with Ben.

It seemed incredible to be back in the Western Port area. It had only been 15 years earlier, that I had been a self-confessed atheist and a broken alcoholic with suicidal thoughts. I was blinded to the truth by a spiritual enemy I hadn't believed existed and was now pastoring a church full of people that were all walking their own journey of triumph and challenge. It seemed I had come full circle.

Chapter 11 CHANGE & PROPHECY

Hastings was a lower socio-economic, working-class community which (at that time), suffered higher than average rates of crime, substantial drug and alcohol-related family violence issues, child abuse, and teen suicide. We were in a literal life-and-death battle for the souls of this community. I knew I was powerless in my strength to fight the battle against this very real spiritual enemy, and to save people from these very real situations. But God had called me, and I prayed that as I covered myself in *His armour*, in *His strength*, that He would 'release the wonderful mystery of His hope-filled gospel

(Eph 6:20 TPT) and use me to preach (both by word and lifestyle), His wonderful freedom.

Father's Day Call

The sobbing voice on the other end of the phone said, 'Our son has died in a drowning accident at Mt Martha. Pastor Vic, can you please help?'

It was a Father's Day, neither this family nor I will ever forget, as I left behind my family to take these shocked, grieving parents to identify their 19-year-old son's body at the Melbourne City Morgue.

As our church loved on this grieving family and offered support, it seemed inadequate for the heartache and despair they were suffering. I dug deep into the Bible, God's Word, for only there could I find words of hope and comfort to help this broken-hearted family.

The Bible says that the Holy Spirit, is the great Comforter and Counsellor, and He seemed to come right alongside this family. We felt His tangible presence, as the words of Jesus Christ were spoken over this teenager's coffin at his funeral. Even at this sad time, the Holy Spirit through God's Word reminded all of us of the wonderful hope of heaven; a life beyond this short time on earth - eternal life, and the hope that one day, would be reunited.

***

The Accident

Does it get any better than this? I felt like the richest man on Earth, not with worldly wealth usually associated with expensive toys and plenty of cash to splash; I certainly didn't have that! It was with priceless Godly contentment.

It was one of those rare moments in the busyness of life with all its challenges, when I had what I refer to as, a 'love burst' for God as I began reflecting on the many blessings, we'd received from Him.

I had a great marriage and was madly in love with my wife, Lindy, who is my soul mate and best friend. Christ's love for us was so real that we could not but help share that love with others. We had a particular fondness and care for those who struggled with the challenges of blended families and friends.

We often say to people that we met in the second-hand shop, and now, by the grace of God, we are born again – or made new. Old things are brand new (John 3:3, 2; Cor 5:17 NKJV). Together, we were on this amazing journey, and even though we had both been broken and lost and had despaired of life, God had caused our paths to meet.

It was March 1999, and we were thoroughly enjoying pastoring in Hastings. It was one of those beautiful autumn mornings as I drove across to visit my mum, who was at Rye on the Port Philip Bay side of the peninsula. The 40-minute drive takes in some beautiful countryside and stunning sea views as you head into Flinders or over Arthurs Seat, looking down and across Port Philip Bay.

Chapter 11   CHANGE & PROPHECY

Mum had attended some of our church meetings and certain marriage ceremonies that I had performed for family members. I was always encouraged by her presence. She was not a churchgoer, and I don't think she even had a bible, so what I learnt from her that day, absolutely blew my mind! My father had vaguely told me of an accident that had nearly killed me when I was small, but I never knew the details. My mum understandably hadn't talked about the details either, but on this particular day, for whatever reason, she decided to share her version of the horrific event with me. When I left her that day, I was reminded that God truly is an all-knowing God!

Our start of mother-son conversation began as usual as we settled down to visit. We swapped the telling on current news going on in our worlds, and then the conversation changed dramatically.

I never saw the truck coming. Mum said we were almost across the street when it came speeding up on the inside lane. To this day, I don't remember. But I do remember the look of anguish on my mother's face as she re-lived that historic moment all over again. It was like she was there. As she sat across the table from her 48- year son, she was transported back in time. For me, time stood still as she began to speak.

It was a beautiful autumn day (much like my present-day), in Melbourne on Tuesday 11th April 1950, I was sixteen months old. Mum had decided to take me for a walk around the block while Nanna looked after baby Lyn.

We often walked places as Mum didn't have a car. Mum took her normal route, and as usual, we went to cross Ingles Street, Port Melbourne, completely oblivious to the speeding truck coming our way. It happened so fast! Mum lifted her eyes from her smiling boy, but too late! My mother was powerless to do anything but see this awful nightmare come to pass right in front of her eyes. It would only last seconds, but to her, it felt like an eternity.

The speeding truck complete with a drunk driver and large front bumper bar, connected with her little boy, throwing me meters away from her. I was head high to the front bumper bar, my face taking most of the impact. Mum was also hit, but she was carrying a blanket over her arm and only had bad bruising; but was more worried about me.

The force of the impact caused severe head and facial lacerations that would forever leave its scar as well as a broken leg. In a heartbeat, I went from a lively and energetic toddler going for a walk, to a motionless, bloodied bundle of pulp on the side of the road. The truck driver eventually stopped but was so drunk he could barely stand up straight.

The nightmare continued as the Ambulance Service of the day was not as it is now. There were no sirens, and there was no on-scene first-aid. A bystander gathered my broken body from the road and yelled to the drunken driver, 'You've done this, you mongrel! Take them to the hospital!' He ushered us into the utility with this drunk driver and headed for the emergency department. My mum described the ride to Prince Henry Hospital as 'hair-raising!

In a twist of irony, Mum and Dad learnt later that the man who had lifted me off the street was a local burglar named Bill Sykes. He went from villain to hero as Mum and Dad invited him home and gave a party to thank him for his swift action that likely saved my life.

At the Prince Henry Hospital, I was rushed straight into emergency. Because Mum only had bruising, she was told to go home to baby Lyn as she was breastfeeding (the customs were different then). My life was left in the hands of the surgeons.

Chapter 11   CHANGE & PROPHECY

The Prophecy

After returning home to Nanna's and baby Lyn, Mum, still shocked from the horror of it all, sobbed uncontrollably and was sick with worry for her little boy. She didn't know if he would survive or live with permanent brain damage.

As she was sitting in the front room nursing baby Lyn who had fallen asleep in her arms, Nanna's neighbour and friend (a spiritual lady), dropped by and gently spoke words of encouragement to Mum that she believed were from God.

"Your little boy Victor is not going to die. You will hear the pattering of his little feet running up and down this passage. God has plans for his life – to serve Him!"

Mum saw the first part of the prophecy come true as I lived and eventually ran up and down Nan's passages again, but not until after I'd spent a long time in hospital. There were many follow-up visits to x-ray as the excessive build-up of scar tissue on my face and scalp, as I was a 'keloid grower.' (Keloid scarring happens where this is an overgrowth of dense fibrous tissue. It usually develops after an injury has healed and extends beyond the original wound). The visit was tricky with a toddler, as they applied a lead mask, leaving only the scar tissue exposed to the dangerous x-ray treatment.

The newspaper of the day reported the 118 stitches it took for the surgeon to sew my face back together again, and my leg injuries left me knocked kneed for life. *I should have died! But God had another plan.*

'God had plans for his life – to serve Him'. It was many years before my Mum saw the second part of the lady's prophecy come true. Mum had hidden this prophecy in her heart for 48 years, how she must've of been tempted to dismiss those words as nonsense, particularly as I aged from 16 to 33. What irony that it was a drunk driver who

nearly took my life, and that for a time, I had chosen that lifestyle too.

I never condone or excuse the actions during that time of my life. It was but by God's grace that I didn't hurt anyone as I had been hurt. God had a plan and purpose for my life, and He was now using me in the same way Nanna's next-door neighbour bought encouragement and God's word to my Mum. I too, now have the opportunity to encourage and share His Word to others going through difficult times. I love the teachings of the Apostle Paul to the Church at Ephesus:

"But God, is so rich in mercy, and He loved us so much, that even though we were dead because of our sins, He gave us life when He raised Christ from the dead (It is only by God's grace that you are saved), and raised us up together, and made us sit together in the heavenly places in Christ Jesus." (Eph. 2:4–6)

I often reflect on the words the Apostle Paul said to a young Timothy in the Bible, "I thank Christ Jesus, our Lord, who has given me strength, that He considered me trustworthy, appointing me to His service. Even though I was once a blasphemer and a persecutor and a violent man, I was shown mercy because I acted in ignorance and unbelief. The grace of our Lord was poured out on me abundantly, along with the faith and love that are in Christ Jesus." (1 Timothy 1:12-14 NIV).

These words described who I once was, and I'm in awe and wonder that God now uses me! I thank Jesus who truly saved me (in every sense of the word) and then enabled me to return to Hastings, healthy and whole, with a happy marriage and the privilege of ministering to others in their time of need.

"He heals the broken-hearted and bandages their wounds. He counts the stars and calls them all by name. How great is our Lord! His power is absolute! His understanding is beyond comprehension!" (Psalm 147:3–5).

Chapter 11 CHANGE & PROPHECY

If you're broken-hearted today, and you feel the broken pieces are scattered so far apart, you can't find them; Be encouraged, because I KNOW that if God can save me, He can save you! And God knows where to find the scattered pieces, bring them together and make any heart, no matter how broken, whole again!

Chapter 12

PASSING THE BATON

We had purchased a beautiful old Victorian home and to pay the mortgage, I was working as a sub-contract painter. It was difficult work, but at the time the only work I could get, so I was grateful for the income. By now, we had been pastoring at the Hastings church for over 12 months. I was down on my knees painting a skirting board in a newly built house; it was a stinking hot day with sweat dripping off my nose, and I had the sorest of knees when the phone rang, *it was a call of change.*

The call came from a lady named Jody. She and her husband Mark had been youth leaders at Frankston Community Church and were now program directors at Teen Challenge's residential rehabilitation farm in rural Victoria. 'We need someone to pastor our church on the Teen Challenge farm property in Kyabram, Victoria, and we believe God has prompted us to ask if *you'll* take it on.'

While I did have an excitement in my spirit and began thanking God with tears of joy that He had been mindful of us, I had a lot of questions. What about the church at Hastings? Who was going to pastor them if we left? What about our recently purchased home? How is Lindy going to feel about leaving her home, again?

I believe God used us as a link in a chain of succession for the future of the church at Hastings. We had received the baton from Pastor Len who had within a few years, not only been effective in reaching unchurched kids through the many outreach children's programs but had managed to purchase the Hastings AOG Church's first property in King Street, Hastings. It is a financial and spiritual legacy on which the church is still flourishing today.

In hindsight, we were the interim while God was preparing someone else, who would once again forge new territory for the church and position the church to be of greater benefit to the community of Hastings. Our time there was short, we never planned it that way, but God knew. It was now time for us to pass the baton on, but onto whom?

We had dropped off some of our youth for a meeting, and we were sitting in our vehicle. I turned to Euan, who was our church treasurer and a long-time friend, and informed him that I believed God had called us to Teen Challenge at Kyabram. I explained to him how I had prayed and asked God, 'What about the Hastings church? Who is going to pastor them?' As clear as a bell going off in my head, I believe God communicated to me, *'It's time for Euan to step up to the plate.'*

I think the colour in his face came back after a while and I continued, 'Mate, I'm sorry to shock you, but I think you should ask God yourself. Let us know what you hear.'

Pastor Euan and his wife Carolyn, after realising it was God's call to action, they took on the leadership of the now Harbourside Church. God blessed their leadership, and the church experienced great success with their youth group and the newly created charity arm of Habourcare. It wasn't long before they realised that they were quickly outgrowing the King Street facility for Sunday services and Harbourcare required more space.

Using their real estate background and entrepreneurial skills and with much prayer and planning, they sold the King Street property and were able to purchase and renovate the much larger facility at the now growing and vibrant church's new location in Bray Street, Hastings. The baton had been passed on!

***

War Zone

2001 was a year of highs and lows for us, of challenge and jubilation. It was a time of learning and being moulded and shaped on what the Bible refers to as the 'potter's wheel', as God fashioned and formed us through clay and refiner's fire taking us into the deeper things of God and His Kingdom's purposes. Sound painful? Oh, yes!

We were in a war zone! It was literally a life-and-death battle. As pastor of the church on the property of the Teen Challenge Centre, Lindy's and my mission was to reach young people caught up in drug and alcohol abuse, pornography, gambling and many other life-controlling issues, including Satanic ritual abuse, with the Holy Spirit-empowered, life-transforming Gospel of Jesus Christ.

Dammed if I do

Established in 1974, Teen Challenge Victoria started as a non-residential Christian counselling centre in the city suburb of St Kilda. It was predominantly for male students, but females also attended. It soon became evident there was a need to get students into a long-term residential program following the success of these types of TC programs in the US and other parts of the world.

TC bought a property at Kyabram in Victoria's Goulburn Valley. The 40-acre site they purchased had been a fruit block with the pickers' huts still intact. It also had a couple of farmhouses and a large dam at the rear which TC had been fortunate enough to acquire.

The inaugural long-term residential students were all males and happily stayed in the converted pickers' huts that were affectionately known as 'The Bronx', so named after the South Bronx, which saw a sharp decline in population, liveable housing and quality of life in the late 1960s and 1970s, culminating in a wave of arson. Later, we took on female students as well.

I had the privilege of water baptising many students at TC. In the early days, we used the on-site muddy dam complete with yabbies, snakes and leeches. During our time there were able to add to the chapel, a galvanised baptismal tub filled with warmed clean bore water.

Many times, there wouldn't be a dry eye, as 'trophies of grace' courageously told their stories of being delivered out of terrible circumstances of human degradation. They told how they'd felt confused, alone and bankrupt mentally, physically and financially. They'd hated who they had become because of childhood physical and sexual abuse and self-harm. Some had even survived multiple suicide attempts.

Many shared how, to escape from their emotional pain, they had experimented with drugs, alcohol and illicit sex, gambling, over-eating, which led to bulimia, or they developed anorexia. For a brief time, they found relief but soon had to increase the use of their drug of choice to maintain their feeling of euphoria and escape from reality.

With great thankfulness to God, I share the following stories of some of those who were part of the TC family that God had allowed me to be a part of their journey. I had the privilege of witnessing their life change from life-controlling addiction to experiencing God's love, mercy, and saving grace. Whom went on to live with the assurance of eternal life through the power of the Holy Spirit and the revelation that God has a plan and purpose for everyone regardless of their past. *Note: Because of the personal nature, their names are changed to respect their privacy.*

Chapter 12 PASSING THE BATON

Bridgett's Story

Bridgett shared that she had never known her dad. As a little girl, her alcoholic mother had many boyfriends over and would lock her in a cupboard when they came around. As she grew into her teens, she started drinking and taking drugs, going from one boyfriend to another. She was looking for love to fill the void in her young life that had only known abuse and rejection.

Her life seemed to be a rollercoaster, with the highs and lows of her rapidly increasing expensive drug addiction. She couldn't hold down a job and began shoplifting to pay for drugs, eventually resorting to prostitution.

One day she met Brad, who was a drug-addicted teenage alcoholic who she loved. Brad introduced her to train surfing, which she found daring and exciting, but she didn't think about the danger because they were together.

Brad was instantly killed when he slipped off a fast-moving train after his head hit the railway infrastructure. Bridgett was broken-hearted after losing the only person she believed had loved her. She took a carving knife to her stomach in a self-harming suicide attempt.

The detective who was at her bedside in the hospital, after she recovered from emergency surgery, asked her about her boyfriend's tragic train-surfing death. Bob, a detective sergeant, was a Christian who, along with his wife and family, attended what we called a gatehouse church for TC. These churches had personnel trained to not only physically help, encourage and pray for people where possible but to interview those who had expressed a desire to deal with their life-controlling problems at our residential program at Kyabram.

He was God's provision for Bridgett, as he shared with her that 'God loves you unconditionally'. It wasn't just a throwaway line; he backed it up by offering to let a homeless Bridgett stay with him and his wife and family. Eventually, after her physical body recovered, she came to us at TC, where she received the fullness of God's love after committing her life to Christ Jesus. She was water baptised and completed the TC program and internship. She was healed and free.

Benjamin

Peter and Nancy met in Singapore. Peter, who had been a drug addict for many years, had hit rock bottom and cried out for help. After being referred to TC in Singapore, where he completed the program. He too experienced the fullness of God's love and accepted Jesus as Lord of his life and saviour. He and his then-new Chinese Singaporean wife, Nancy, dedicated themselves to helping others overcome life-controlling addiction. Peter and Nancy transferred from TC Singapore to work with us at TC Kyabram in Victoria.

Benjamin, their first child, was a beautiful little boy who delighted the hearts of his parents. They felt he was God's blessing to them after many failed attempts to get pregnant.

Sadly, Benjamin's fight for life ended after he spent most of the eight months of his life in the children's hospital in Melbourne. Down syndrome and many other medical complications in his little body took a toll on their precious only child. These devastated parents, along with many of us at TC, had called out to God for a miracle of healing. Why didn't God heal him? Why did God give him to us and then take him from us? These and many other questions haunted these grieving parents and many of us in our close TC family.

They were understandably overwhelmed by feelings of shock, sadness, denial and anger. As their pastor, I couldn't answer questions to which only God knew the answers.

Chapter 12 PASSING THE BATON

Like many parents who have lost a child, they will never understand the unanswered haunting 'why' questions this side of eternity.

The tiny white coffin was gently placed on the stage in our chapel and lovingly adorned with beautiful flowers as we worshipped God and celebrated Benjamin's brief life on Earth. While the questions may always linger, we were able to thank God for the *hope of heaven,* knowing that one day there will be a joyful reunion for Peter and Nancy. Peter and Nancy had raised children from many other parents to a place of hope and safety. Now God would do the same for their son Benjamin.

Cheryl, a Coincidence?

It was a Monday morning and one of the workers, Phil, on the TC programs joined me in taking Monty, our miniature terrier dog, for a walk beside the irrigation channel along South Boundary Road. We met a woman we didn't know who was also walking her dog. 'Are you from Teen Challenge?' she asked.

She mentioned that she'd just met a young mum named Cheryl in the Kyabram Hospital. 'She's not well, and I'm very concerned about her. Will you please pray for her at your church?'

> 'Yes, sure will! Do you go to one of the churches in Kyabram township?'
> 'No, I don't go to any church.'

For me, it was one of those God moments when the Holy Spirit had arranged a divine appointment. I've never heard the audible voice of God, but I know when He prompts me with an urgency in my spirit. (*I had experienced this hearing when my mate, big Wayne the Tasmanian axeman, was not well*).

It was only five minutes by car to the Kyabram Hospital. I'd started praying with Phil as we walked back to TC and continued praying in tongues until we arrived at the hospital to visit this woman named Cheryl.

I didn't know her, but Almighty God did, and flung open heaven's doors of grace. After explaining to the hospital receptionist who I was and who I'd wanted to visit, she said, 'You're in luck. There is a Cheryl in bed four just up the passage, who was supposed to be transported an hour ago to Shepparton District Hospital.'

After explaining to Cheryl, the extraordinary sequence of events that had led me to her, I told her how God had prompted my heart to deliver His word and that He was not only mindful of her but truly loved her. I sensed a tangible presence of The Holy Spirit as her sad eyes filled with tears. Her cancer had advanced, and it was terminal, and she willingly received the fullness of God's love into her broken heart and asked Jesus Christ to be her personal Lord and Saviour, receiving forgiveness, salvation, healing, peace and eternal life.

Cheryl exchanged her frail cancer-ridden body for a new perfectly healed body when she passed from this life into eternity. She went into the presence of her Saviour, Jesus Christ, three weeks after what I believe was her divine appointment to receive God's grace through her faith for salvation.

Jason

The rapid knocking on our front door was loud and seemed to have a sense of urgency as we awoke from a deep sleep at 1.00 am Monday. My heart raced as I opened the door to a panic-stricken, concerned intern who was on duty. 'It's Jason. We can't seem to wake him!'

Chapter 12   PASSING THE BATON

Jason shared one of the converted fruit pickers' huts with another male student who had been trying to wake him without any success. He soon realised he wasn't breathing and rushed over to notify the duty intern and then began CPR on him.

The ambulance officers were there in five minutes and worked on him for 20 minutes before taking him to Kyabram Hospital. By this time, most of the students and resident workers, having heard the news, had gathered in the chapel, where we prayed for healing.

Tragically, a couple of hours later, 26-year-old Jason was pronounced dead. We later found out that while on his second weekend at home after successfully not using drugs or alcohol on his first weekend of leave, he had used drugs and sneaked some back into TC, where he had overdosed on Oxycodone, a morphine-based drug often administered in palliative care for those with a terminal illness. He had self-medicated and fallen into a comatose sleep until, sadly, his young heart had stopped beating.

Jason was a bright, talented young man who had, at one time, trained as a light aircraft pilot. His fellow students and the staff workers at TC thought highly of him, and he seemed to join in wholeheartedly with the praise and worship at our mid-week and Sunday church services. He wasn't from a dysfunctional family like some other students. He'd come to TC referred from a gatehouse church that his family attended in one of country Victoria's regional centres.

It didn't make sense that a life that offered so much potential could be taken away. His family, who loved him, had tried so hard to help their son get off drugs and were broken-hearted and devastated and felt that they had failed as parents. As their Pastor, I was broken-hearted!

I can only imagine the temptation to take drugs on that second weekend, so convincing to this young man that he couldn't resist. He had previously experienced and become addicted to the euphoria and temporary relief he received from mental and physical pain and the fleeting moment of peace that drugs gave him.

This is an illustration of the way I believe our spiritual enemy, Satan, the father of lies, works his deceivings and temptations. I believe because as I look back in hindsight, I know I heard that same voice. That incessant loud voice of condemnation, 'You're no good. You're a loser!' At your lowest point, he'll kick you in the guts by recalling all the bad things you've said and done, all the negative words said about you and the hurtful actions inflicted on you that you've experienced throughout your life.

In the other ear, it's a temptation that's conjured up to lure you into a trap. A wonderful picture comes into your mind of exotic pleasure in a utopia that you can never get to because it's a mirage. If chocolate is your weak point, it would be the world's best, beautifully presented, and free of charge; but it would cost you your life. Why? It's chocolate-coated arsenic. It looks good and tastes fantastic until you get to the deadly centre.

Sadly Jason had listened to the false lie of the enemy. I say this with no condemnation whatsoever, because I too, had heard the voice and knew the temptation, but by God's Grace!

Our time at Teen Challenge was tumultuous in many ways and certainly stretched us in our faith. God had been working through us to minister to others. It's humbling and gratifying that the Holy Spirit would move through us. We can't save everyone, but God never slumbers or takes a vacation. He is constantly working on us and through us. He did call Lindy and me to serve both these churches, and pain and all, we are so grateful.

God raised up another to lead the TC chapel and family and once again, it was time for us to pack up and pass on the baton.

Chapter 12 PASSING THE BATON

As I reflect on my time in both Hastings Church and Kyabram, and I consider the beautiful but broken people God had placed in our path to assist, I stand in awe again of all that God saved me from, and now uses me to bring his love and mercy into the lives of others. I'm encouraged that Jason *had received Jesus Christ as his Saviour and Lord and had been baptised by water. His salvation and a place in God's heaven were assured because he accepted the work done by Jesus Christ on Calvary's Cross.*

"God saved you by his grace when you believed. And you can't take credit for this; it is a gift from God. Salvation is not a reward for the good things we have done, so none of us can boast about it. For we are God's masterpiece. He has created us anew in Christ Jesus, so we can do the good things he planned for us long ago." (Eph 2:8–10)

The devil's methods haven't changed since the beginning of creation way back in Genesis, where he brings deception to Adam and Eve. He is real, and deception is his greatest tool, and he'll use anything he can to bring deceit. But his way is not the way, and God purposes you for so much more than you'll ever know than you'll imagine for yourself. He's certainly shown that true to me. I never imagined that I would be one day serving a God that I didn't even believe in!

Challenge and pain are still part of life, but regardless of my past or your past, God is not limited by our limitations, and I am not dependant on my strength and knowledge alone. So I serve Him with my life and leave the rest to Him.

"Now to Him who is able to do exceedingly abundantly above all that we ask or think according to the power that works in us..." *Eph 3:20 NKJV*

Chapter 13

GROWING PAINS

We began as lead pastors at Carrum Downs Community Care Church and ministered there for around 13 years. Many times, during those 13 years we'd have gladly taken early retirement just to run away, especially during the dreaded church split.

One of our leaders who was overseeing the not-for-profit ministry of the church had been encouraged to separate this ministry from the church and run it independently, sadly though, several people in our church went with him.

Division and animosity in church life are not necessarily new, as we're all imperfect people; it even happened way back in the first church with Paul and Barnabas -Acts 15:36–41. But I've learnt that while we might have had a painful disagreement over personnel and ministry direction, it doesn't have to end the love and what we had for one another. Just as Paul and Barnabas moved on from sharp dispute for the greater good, we both did too in time.

I don't like confrontation, and this shook us right to the core of our being. We loved the people that God had called us to lead, so for people to leave us was heart-breaking. My default had been and to some extent still is, that, when I'm under the pump, I escape (no longer by boozing but by running away). I handed in my resignation, but the board were adamant. 'No way! We want you to stay.' B*ummer*!

While we were greatly encouraged that we were still wanted, the exit had closed. Looking back, this was God's grace for us and proved to be a watershed moment in our ministry. Once I began to face up to my failures and shortcomings, I began to pray desperately asking God for wisdom and direction. Another reminder to lean on God's strength and understanding and not my own.

My years as a lead pastor up to that point had been just following along with previous methodology stereotyping, going the same way others had led churches, even though they'd had different gifts/talents. I fell way short. But the truth is, 'comparison is the thief of joy'. The lesson I'm still learning and growing into is to be comfortable in my God-given gifts!

I always tried to be fair dinkum about forgiveness. My spiritual litmus test for genuine forgiveness is that I fervently pray for those who have hurt or disappointed me, not in a one-off religious prayer, but ongoing for them, their families and even in some cases, their new church. Jesus teaches us:

But to you who are willing to listen, I say, love your enemies! Do good to those who hate you. Bless those who curse you. Pray for those who hurt you. (Luke 6:27–28)

My prayer for wisdom and direction was answered. The cavalry turned up, and the ACC district leaders graciously helped all parties concerned to embrace forgiveness and, over time, healing and reconciliation.

Connect and Engage

While it has been an incredibly tough time, I realised that running away was *not* an option (albeit tempting), and understandably, our confidence was shaken. With encouragement received both from the remnant of people who stayed, as well as our long-time friend and mentor, Ps Ian, we decided that it was time to move forward and continue to give our best with the faithful people to which God had called us.

Chapter 13 GROWING PAINS

We weren't the shakers and movers of Christianity with a star-studded cast of ministries, just faithful plodders who were willing to learn and step up to the plate and have a go. Together as Community Care Church, we embraced the vision to connect and engage with our community whoever, wherever, whatever—work, sport, social, family, friends, all undergirded by prayer and praise testimonies, giving glory to God.

We were punching way above our weight as our comparatively small church effectively facilitated and hosted suicide awareness prevention seminars, secondary school breakfasts, nursing home ministries, marriage ceremonies and tutoring. We also helped many Sudanese families within our community with education and integration issues.

On one occasion, our church was able to play a part in uniting a family separated through the war in Southern Sudan.

Elizabeth and six of her children had hurriedly escaped their hometown in Southern Sudan ahead of the returning Muslim soldiers who had killed her husband and many other men from her village. Their best hope for survival was to send the older teenage children and their cousins one way while Elizabeth and the little ones went in the opposite direction.

They fled on foot with little food and clothing, but this brave Christian mum and the four little ones, including a baby and a disabled polio victim with a severe limp, managed to endure the dangerous 28-day journey across the bottom of Southern Sudan into neighbouring Kenya.

They finally arrived at Kakuma Refugee Camp, which served refugees who were forcibly displaced from their home countries due to war or persecution. The camp was a small city of thatched-roof huts, tents and mud abodes. Living inside the camp was equally prison and exile, and certainly not a holiday camp! Elizabeth and the four youngest children endured the hardships and were *eventually* granted refugee visas to enter Australia three years after fleeing their home in Nuer.

This dear lady that had been through so much heartbreak, losing her husband and other family members, and couldn't rest with the uncertainty. She had to know if her two teenage children, Nyabol and Mandet and their cousins, were still alive somewhere in Africa. Elizabeth's prayers were answered, when she received the good news that they were alive and well. They had survived many perilous situations, and found their way to the UNHCR refugee camp in Kakuma, Kenya, only to discover their mum and siblings were in Australia.

After two years, many meetings about applications, refusals, tears, disappointments and much prayer, we received what I believe was God's miraculous provision of an immigration lawyer, who tirelessly worked pro bono until they finally had their visas to come to Australia. And our church family was privileged to play a part in and witness what they had all been praying for the two years it took to get them to Australia and through the doors of our church.

It was an amazing sight! I'll never forget as a six-foot-eight Mandet and his younger sister, Nyabol, embraced their mother and the siblings they hadn't seen for five years. Elizabeth was overjoyed and, with tears flowing down her cheeks and with her arms raised to God, kept repeating the Nuer words for happy or joyful heart unto God Almighty—'*Teeth Loach Da! Teeth Loach Da!*'

The Final Baton Pass

Our season at Community Care Church did end up coming to a close, and we retired as the lead pastors and passed on the baton one final time. We have again made our home a little past Hastings, and are back to serving (in our retired way), now at Hastings Connect Christian Church. We are surrounded by a great church family, part of a growing campus of Frankston's Connect Christian Church. Once known as *Frankston Community Church*, where we began our discipleship with Ps Ian over 30 years earlier. We consider ourselves privileged that God continues to use us in unexpected ways, and we continue to serve Him until the day He calls us home.

The Apostle Paul points out that it doesn't matter to God how talented you are by the world's proud standard. It's a God thing. The truth is that 'God opposes the proud but favours the humble.' Through these incredible years at this church there were many times of both humbling ourselves before God, and not knowing what the outcome would be, or the next step to take or how we would endure the people hurt. James 4:6 holds true –

"Take a good look, friends, at who you were when you were called into this life. I don't see many of "the brightest and the best" among you, not many influential, not many from high-society families. Isn't it obvious that God deliberately chose men and women that the culture overlooks and exploits and abuses, chose these "nobodies" to expose the hollow pretensions of the 'somebodies'?

I never considered myself to be the brightest and the best, and the battle of comparison perhaps is still yet to be won. But God used what little both Lindy and I had to offer, and the combined skill, hearts and prayers of our little church family, to do a miracle. Imagine if we had run away, we would've missed God's miracle! It wasn't the size of what we had to offer, nor the size of our church that mattered; it was the limitless size of an All-Powerful God working through us!

Chapter 14

FAMILY

The Missing Link

It was Boxing Day, 2012, and Mum was staying with us in Hastings, as she had for many years at Christmastime. She surprised me when she said, 'Vic, when I die, I want you to do my funeral.' Her words shocked me!

> 'Mum, that's a tough gig! If I know you're a Christian, I will.'
> 'You've got no worries, son,' she replied.

I didn't comment any further and took it as encouragement that she was a Christian. But I wondered if, when the time came, if I would be able to hold it together emotionally. She was 87 and in good health. She enjoyed going to her local gym and joining many other social activities at the retirement village where she loved living. I thought she would live to be 100 and receive an acknowledgement from Buckingham Palace!

After having a bad fall, Mum required a pacemaker and never quite recovered the health she had enjoyed for most of her 87 years. I had an inkling that Mum's time on earth was perhaps coming to an end faster than I would like. I worried some as I wasn't 100% convinced that my mother understood Jesus and His eternity. But in the last days of our many early morning phone conversations, and two days before she died, God bought assurance to me. After we prayed together on the phone, she said to me, 'I *knew* Jesus long before you, Vic!'

Those words were not only a huge encouragement for me at the time, with Mum being sick and frail, but seemed to be the missing link between what she had shared in the years after she had first told me of the prophecy spoken to her after the accident that nearly killed me. 'Your little boy, Victor, is not going to die. You will hear the pattering of his little feet running up and down this passage. God has plans for his life to serve Him.'

Mum was an honest, wise lady with great discernment and could sniff out a con merchant in a heartbeat! She didn't like being taken for a fool but would be helpful and encouraging if she felt the person was fair dinkum.

In the years after relating the prophecy to me, and then seeing it fulfilled in my life, she began to share with me, when she realised I would be interested, about the many times she as a girl went with 'Old Gran' to the Pentecostal revival meetings. She joined in with the happy clapping and hallelujahs at the Good News Hall in Queensbury Street near where they lived in North Melbourne.

Mum loved Old Gran (Sarah Ross), who had lived with her when she was a young girl. Sarah had migrated with her family to Australia in the 1850s from Inverness in Scotland. They were pioneer farmers around Warrnambool in the western district of Victoria.

Mum had told us when we were kids, of the brave pioneering adventures Old Gran had told her. After Old Gran's husband died, she would, out of necessity, travel many perilous miles alone by horse and buggy, to buy and sell livestock for the family farm in the male-dominated Newmarket Saleyards, north of Melbourne.

At my mother's funeral, I was privileged to eulogise and celebrate her life. This great lady was a true-blue Aussie battler with a Scottish heritage. I shared the good news confidently with our family and friends, as encapsulated in John's Gospel, John 3:16.

In God's love, mercy, and saving grace He not only received Mum into heaven for eternity, but had prepared my heart and emboldened my faith. He had blessed my Mum with enough years to see the prophecy outlive the years of my life, that she must've of doubted so many times. And the missing link was found, with both of us connected to Almighty God for eternity. I had prayed and believed for Mum's salvation for well over 30 years. I believe, this was God's plan from the beginning.

God's Endless Grace

I am so grateful to God that he has blessed me with a wonderful family. I will forever carry the scars of regret for having missed the opportunity through my selfishness to be a loving husband to Jean, and a real father to our four wonderful kids Shane, Karen, Leanne, and Brendan during their young years.

My decisions inadvertently had robbed them of a childhood with a Father who should've been there for them, and they too have scars that I'll never be able to take away. But God is a gracious God, and I've had the privilege now, to look back with a 'love burst to God moment', as I continue to experience the result of the wonderful healing and restoration of relationships that have blossomed and bloomed with *all* of our family over many years.

Our now-adult children that I love so very much, have been very gracious and forgiving to love me, and have allowed me to be 'Dad' again. They've also given me the honour to Grandparent the many grandkids I have and even great-grandchildren. And, I've even been able be 'Pa' to Lindy's grandchildren too.

Christmas time, in particular, Boxing Day, was hosted for many years in our family home and now the tradition continues in my daughter's home. It's an all-in family time for Lindy and me. Even Jean and her son Tom for many years, have been and continue to be, loving friends and family, that join our all-inclusive family celebrations.

What an incredible journey my life ended up being and continues to be. I love God and continue to serve Him through the power of The Holy Spirit. I was once a lost, sin-sick, depraved human who had lost all his family. But now I'm blessed with restored relationship with my children, and my children's children; I have a great church family that love and care for Lindy and I. AND, I have been adopted into God's family with the assurance of eternal life in heaven. God calls me, Son!

Although I cannot have the years of my youth again, God has more than made up for those years eaten away by alcohol, bad decisions and resulted devastation. Despite all that passed, God in His endless grace has dealt wondrously with me!

"And I will compensate you for the years that the swarming locust has eaten...You will have plenty to eat and be satisfied and praise the Name of the Lord your God who had death wondrously with you; (Joel 2:25 &26 AMP)

I can never repay God for his love and undeserved favour which was showered upon me through Jesus Christ's work on the cross. I remain eternally grateful to Him for extricating me from death row and paying for my massive debt of sin! What He has given me and restored back to me is immeasurable.

"God can do anything, you know—far more than you could ever imagine, or guess or request in your wildest dreams! He does it not by pushing us around but by working within us, his Spirit deeply and gently within us." Eph 3.20-21 MSG

Chapter 15

I AM ARRESTED!

"What if there is a God and you could meet Him?"

That was the question that Bill had asked me long ago and was now clanging in my ear like a loud bell. After being sober for a few weeks, there was a curiosity in my mind, especially after Bill, who seemed sane and sincere, explained how he had felt when he'd had his *encounter* with God (through the Holy Spirit), describing the feeling as 'better than having sex!'

I wanted that experience, something that would stimulate all five senses, and that would dull every other sound or thought. I knew nothing in the area of faith, only as what people referred to as a kind of 'sixth sense'. Faith was outside my comfort zone. It felt awkward and weird.

I had heard of the paranormal with ghosts, witches, devils and angels, but I had thought they were fairy tales! UFOs and aliens seemed more plausible! The meaning of life was something that scientists were to figure out, perhaps life even on other planets. My ignorant atheistic thoughts had me completely blind to the spiritual realm.

"Satan, who is the god of this world, has blinded the minds of those who don't believe. They are unable to see the glorious light of the Good News. They don't understand this message about the glory of Christ, who is the exact likeness of God." (2 Corinthians 4:4)

I didn't understand faith and had total disregard for the spiritual realm. I didn't believe in God, but God Almighty (also known as "I AM") knew what was required for Victor Charles Krone to become connected to Him and *He* had a plan and purpose for my life.

As I look back on that first encounter, I can understand why, for me, there was no wonderful 'feeling'. My cry out to God was more a desperate, silent *scream* for help, and to a God, I had previously decided didn't even exist.

On that night, I was wrestling with suicidal thoughts that were offering a quick escape from the mental anguish and utter despair I had fallen into as a result of living life the way I did. This prayer, (if you could call it that), was only a millisecond thought process that went out from my screwed-up mind, transcending through layers of atheistic unbelief directly to God's ears. *Somehow,* it bypassed the *other* invitation presented to me, with a clear picture and enticing surround sound; the words, *'Put the gun into your mouth, squeeze the trigger and you'll be at peace.'*

If you could measure faith, mine was in the DNA form, microscopic! Yet, it was enough, and God amazingly rewarded it. Unlike Bill, I didn't have the wonderful feeling he described, nor the bolt of lightning I thought it could be like, but the miracle was - there *was* a 'next morning', and it was different!

I awoke that morning, same as any morning, with feelings of dread and fear, but instead of reaching for the 'hair of the dog', I rang Bill, who had offered to help with any 'alcohol-related' problems.

Unknown to me at the time, that moment of prayer was a moment of exercised faith towards God. And that was all He needs to start *anyone* on the journey that He has purposed for them before the foundation of the world.

Even before God made the world, God loved us and chose us in Christ to be holy and without fault in his eyes.

Chapter 15   I AM ARRESTED!

When sin entered the world, there was a gap between God and us that could only be bridged one way. But God being all-knowing, had already decided in advance to adopt us into his own family, by bringing us to himself through Jesus Christ. This is what he wanted to do, and it gave him great pleasure. (Eph1:4–5)

When I first decided to exercise my DNA-sized faith, it was a desperate plea for help. My understanding now, is that the second time was enabled by the first time, because by then, God's undeserved favour was on my life, even though my physical feelings weren't stimulated. God knew me and what it would take for me to further enquire, *by faith*, "What if there is a God and you could meet him?"

As I continued the journey of seeking to understand God, and eventually experiencing His love, healing, forgiveness and peace through Christ Jesus, it became evident that this was *His* doing right from the beginning. My life changed from that moment on, the moment I exercised that DNA-sized faith. This truth revealed again and again in small ways throughout my life but most stunningly, after my mum related the prophecy she had hidden in her heart after the accident that nearly took my life. God purposed me!

A very foolish, wilful Victor Krone had been justly and deservedly arrested and locked in jail cells and deprived of what *I thought* freedom was, but now I willingly and undeservedly have been arrested by Almighty God, the great 'I AM'. I was set free to *choose* Jesus Christ as Lord and Saviour, and therefore live out what true freedom is. No longer a slave to sin but adopted by Father God.

Jesus said, "I tell you most solemnly that anyone who chooses a life of sin is trapped in a dead-end life, and is, in fact, a slave. A slave is a transient, who can't come and go at will. The Son, though, has an established position, the run of the house. So, if the Son sets you free, you are free through and through." (John 8:34–36 MSG).

The Bible speaks in Exodus 3:14, about God telling Moses His Name, "I AM". 'I AM who I AM.' It speaks of a God who is self-sufficient, self-existent, all-encompassing, and without limitations, the one being in the universe who is not dependent on something else for His existence.

God, who has all power and all wisdom, had given me a free will, as He has with all humanity. But that doesn't mean I could do whatever I wanted without suffering the consequences. I was responsible for the choices I made. I could choose to plant whatever I wanted, but I couldn't choose what I would harvest.

So, *I AM Arrested!* Arrested by I AM's love and purpose for me, yet free from all that once held me in bondage. *I AM Arrested* to live by faith and trust in a God who I once denied belief, but who never denied me! *I AM Arrested*, detained by God's great grace to fulfil all that He would have me do. *I AM, Arrested!*

What if there is a God and you could meet Him?

As a Christian, all that I am and do today is not centred on my feelings. That doesn't mean I lack emotion or I'm unable to show my feelings. I cry now more than I ever did!

Those feelings of God's encounters that I describe as 'love bursts to God' are infrequent. I would love that feeling *all* the time, but my relationship with God is not based on my feelings. Yes, I can still get angry or have a good belly laugh, but now I'm not afraid to show my gentle nature, and I'm working on the anger bit! Both are a part of the freedom that Christ has given me.

God wants His kids to live by faith (2 Cor 5:7) to trust him (beyond their feelings) and with all their hearts (Prov 3:5-6). It's not blind faith, wishful thinking or some religion that brainwashes you into believing. My eyes have been opened to the truth that is founded on the infallible life-

Chapter 15   I AM ARRESTED!

transforming authoritative Word of God—the Holy Bible and not my ever-changing, easily influenced feelings.

Jesus Christ, who is the living word, said: "Heaven and earth will disappear, but my words will never disappear." **(Mk 13:31)**

If you've read this far, you would have seen where my easily influenced feelings landed me. You may not have been to that dark place (and I hope you never will), but my understanding of God's Word is that, all humanity has adopted a sinful nature that separated us from God and His purposed life for us.

"For everyone has sinned; we all fall short of God's glorious standard." **Romans 3:23**

"For the wages of sin is death (that is, eternal separation from God), but the gift of God is eternal life (life forever) in Christ Jesus, our Lord." **Romans 6.23 NIV**

I'm not a fire and brimstone preacher who tries to frighten the 'hell' out of people; I'm not interested in that, friendship evangelism is how I encountered Jesus. I have experienced what it is like to be separated from God, and it turned out to be hell on earth, and I don't want that for my eternity, and I don't want it for yours!

However, I cannot deny the *truth*. The Bible tells us clearly that there is a price to be paid for sin. It is eternal separation from God and His heaven.

"Everyone has to die once, then face the consequences." **Hebrews 9:27 MSG**

The ***good news*** is that Jesus has paid the price for *your* sin and that of all people. We are saved from our sin's penalty by God's undeserved favour, wonderfully given through the sacrifice of His son, Jesus Christ, 2000 years ago on a cruel Roman cross. And as you've read, His grace doesn't wait until we pass away, it starts from the moment you action that tiny DNA-sized faith.

God's grace cannot be earnt. It is a gift only received by faith. And it only by faith in Jesus Christ that can bridge that gap of separation from God.

"God saved you by his grace when you believed. And you can't take credit for this; it is a gift from God. Salvation is not a reward for the good things we have done, so none of us can boast about it." **(Ephesians 2:8–9**, emphasis added**)**

"God loves you! He will save you when you believe!" **(John 3:16)**

"If you openly declare that Jesus is Lord and believe in your heart that God raised him from the dead, you will be saved. For it is by believing in your heart that you are made right with God, and it is by openly declaring your faith that you are saved. As the Scriptures tell us, anyone who trusts in him will never be disgraced." **(Romans 10:9–11)**

What if there is a God and you could meet Him?

There *is* a God and you *can* meet Him!

The following is known as the 'sinner's prayer'. It's not a flu injection or some magical formula to avoid hell and get a place in heaven. It's a prayer when, prayed with faith, albeit 'DNA-sized', is the channel that connects you to God Almighty. He knows if you're fair dinkum about confessing your sin, asking for forgiveness and turning your life around to follow Jesus Christ as your Lord and Saviour. You can use the words below if you like:

'Dear Lord Jesus, I know that I am a sinner, and I ask for your forgiveness. I believe You died for my sins and rose from the dead. I turn from my sins and invite you to come into my heart and life. I want to trust and follow You as my Lord and Saviour. In Your name, amen.'

If you have prayed this prayer, I sincerely encourage you to let someone know. Like I did, find a church so that you

Chapter 15 I AM ARRESTED!

can be a part of His community. God never intended for you to do life on your own, either. And, regardless of your past or your feelings, or the consequences of your choices; be confident that God has heard your prayer and He sees you and He knows just what you need. Things may not change for you overnight, it's a life-long journey, but if God can do what He did for me, then do not doubt that God can do it for you!

www.ingramcontent.com/pod-product-compliance
Lightning Source LLC
Chambersburg PA
CBHW050315010526
44107CB00055B/2256